Bruce Tegner

Progressive & Prolific Pioneer of Martial Arts

Abdul Rashid, George Rego

DEDICATION

We would like to dedicate this book to the late Bruce Tegner
for his contributions to the world of martial arts

CONTENTS

ACKNOWLEDGMENTS
By George Rego

I would like to acknowledge my student, Monica Johnson Bridges. Monica was helpful in the proofreading and editing of the chapter I authored on Bruce Tegner's legacy. Her eye for detail made the chapter cleaner and sharper than it would have otherwise been. Furthermore, I would like to thank the author for inviting me to contribute to this book. His own prolific efforts are a real contribution to the world of martial arts. I'm honored to collaborate with him once again.

ACKNOWLEDGMENTS
By Abdul Rashid

I would like to acknowledge the following individuals:

- Holly Woolson

- Professor Michael Belzer

- Jim Bregman

- Emil Farkas

- USAdojo

- S Vinaya Kumar

- Raheem Mali

- My parents

The martial arts great Bruce Tegner did not achieve the same recognition as his contemporaries from the same era, such as Donn Draeger, Robert W Smith, Ed Parker, and others. These days, his book collection is relatively unknown, and there is little information available about him. Upon hearing Tegner's name, I became inspired to research him. After gathering as much information as possible, I decided to compile it into a book. In addition to this, I have enlisted my good friend and martial artist, George Rego, to contribute to this writing. Finally, I would like to thank Tegner's niece, Holly Woolson, for contributing to this writing by providing a detailed insight into her uncle's life.

- Abdul Rashid

1 THE TEGNERS

CHAPTER AUTHORED BY ABDUL RASHID

Bruce Tegner was born Harry Arthur Bruce Hawelka at Grant Hospital in Cook County, Chicago, Illinois, USA on October 28, 1929. His parents were Marjorie June Tegner and Harry Willard Hawelka.

Figure 1 Portrait of Bruce when he around 4 (From the personal archives of Bruce Tegner)

Young Bruce learned some basic boxing from his father. He spent much of his childhood in boarding schools.

Figure 2 Bruce and his father working on the speed bag and speed ball (From the personal archives of Bruce Tegner)

Figure 3 Bruce would grow-up to inherit his father's powerful, athletic stature (From the personal archives of Bruce Tegner)

Figure 4 Harry Willard Hawelka, c. 1933 at the age of 31 (From the personal archives of Bruce Tegner)

Figure 5 Marjorie June Tegner, c. 1933 at the age of 22 (From the personal archives of Bruce Tegner)

His mother June started training in Judo under Theodore Shozo Kuwashima. She is said to have been among the first women in the country to earn a third-degree black belt in Judo. Along with that, she was a pioneering member of the Chicago Judo Club.

Figure 6 June Tegner with Shozo Kuwashima (Keehan, John)

Figure 7 Members of the Chicago Judo club, including T. Shozo Kuwashima, second from left and June Tegner (From the personal archives of Bruce Tegner).

Figure 8 Ashbel R. Welch, top left, and T. Shozo Kuwashima, top middle, together with June Tegner (From the personal archives of Bruce Tegner)

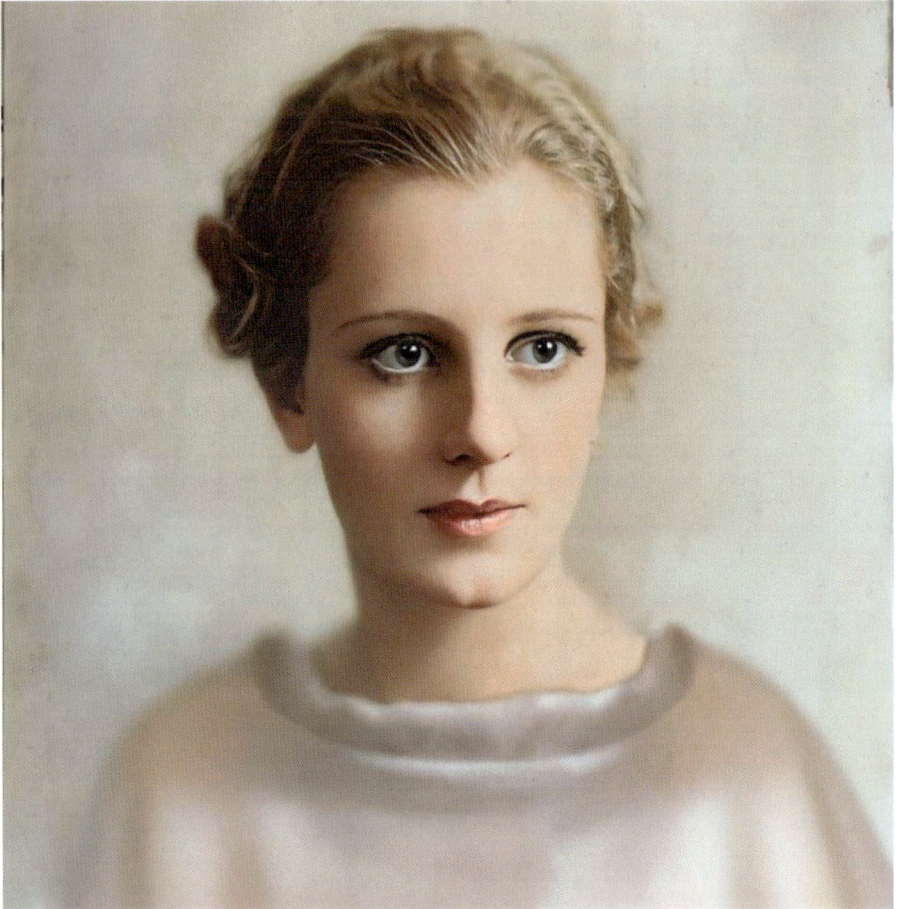

Figure 9 Marjorie June Tegner (From the personal archives of Bruce Tegner)

Figure 10 T. Shozo Kuwashima held a 5th Dan in Judo. He arrived in the United States as a representative of the Kodokan in 1916 and established the first Black Belt Organization in 1920. He acted as head of the New York Dojo for several years. Kuwashima met his demise in 1950. (Self defense Trivandrum)

June later remarried to Jon Tegner. The Tegners operated the club for several years before it was sold to Johnny Osako and Ruth Gardner.

ILLINOIS
Chicago Judo Club
1518 South Michigan Ave., Chicago, Ill.

Figure 11 The Tegner's Judo club as listed on a Judo magazine in 1952 (Carvalho, Danilo)

Figure 12 Joe Alai (top), performing a technique on Jon Tegner (Carvalho, Danilo)

Figure 13 Jon Tegner and professional wrestler, John Madrid (Carvalho, Danilo)

Figure 14 Joe Tegner performing a "Kani Basami" on Edward W. Row of the Lockheed Aircraft Judo Group (Carvalho, Danilo)

"Judo," something new in the art of self-defense, gives June Tegner the upper hand over an obstreperous male. As an expert she demonstrates its triumph of science over brute strength.

Figure 15 June Tegner performs a similar throw during a demonstration. Taken from the "Evening star", October 30, 1938 (Library of Congress)

Another judo trick for dealing with an annoying male—a quick twist of the ankle and he is capsized in this fashion.

Figure 16 June Tegner performing an ankle lock, from the same demonstration (Library of Congress)

Many Hollywood stars, including Humphrey Bogart and Bob Hope, sought technical advice and instruction from the Tegners.

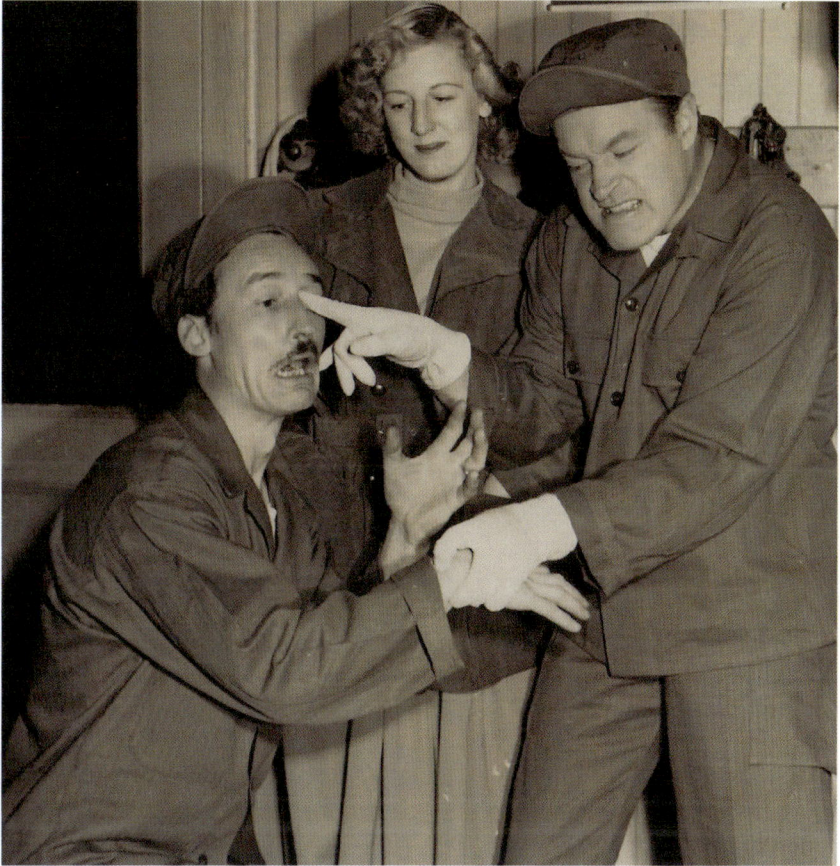

Figure 17 Bob Hope (right), along with June and Jon Tegner. Hope was then preparing for a movie, "Military Policeman" which was released in 1953 (From the personal archives of Bruce Tegner).

Bogart Learns Judo From Woman Expert

HOLLYWOOD — Humphrey Bogart learned Judo for Columbia's "Tokyo Joe," from a 115-pound woman, June Tegner, who can toss Bogey around with great dexterity.

Mrs. Tegner, who sports a "three black belt" rating in Judo competition, has many prominent names among her ex-pupils. She lists actors Gene Kelly and Burgess Meredith; Albert Borden, th milk King; Hastings Harcourt, prominent publisher; and Hollywood bonifce Herman Hover.

Figure 18 A newspaper article about actor Humphrey Bogart learning Judo from June Tegner, taken from the "Toledo union journal", April 22, 1949 (Library of Congress)

HOLLYWOOD, Jan. 21 — (U.P.) — By night she entertains the rich and the famous, by day she tosses 'em over her shoulder and every week she spits on Hollywood from her house atop the city's highest hill.

She's June Tegner, the world's foremost woman judo expert who teaches that art of self-defense to movie folk who want to keep in shape for nitery brawls, tough film assignments or alley sluggings.

You'd think Miss T. would be a hefty Amazon with piano legs and a deep voice. But she's blonde, trim and looks too weak to throw a party, let alone husky men.

At night she's the Pepe Le Moko of the Sunset Strip, the helpless hostess who dishes up cocktails and soft music instead of strangle holds to celebrities like photographer Paul Hesse and composer Harry Ravel.

But don't let those delicate gams and big, blue eyes fool you.

At her judo schools in Chicago, New York, and Hollywood she's thrown to the mat such brave pupils as actor Burgess Meredith; Albert Borden, the milk man; Percy Straus, New York department store magnate, and Publisher Hastings Harcourt.

"Men are afraid to ask me out any more," she signed. "They're afraid I'll break their shoulder blades in a good-night kiss, I guess."

Figure 19 An article about June Tegner and her involvement with Hollywood celebrities, taken from "The Wilmington morning star", January 22, 1947 (Library of Congress)

She said Meredith used to be skeptical of judo until one day when he dared her to break his hold.

"I was afraid I'd hurt him," she said, "but he taunted me until I decided to teach him a lesson. I used a choke hold, which isn't harmful but the victim backs out in a few seconds."

When Meredith came to, she said, he stomped out of the judo school with his tongue hanging out and didn't come back for two years.

"He showed up at my house last week and said he was ready for some more lessons," she grinned.

Special Course

Another Tegner pupil was Herman Hover, the owner of Ciro's nightclub, which is a mile east of June's house as a crow flies.

"When he enrolled in my school I remembered the dough I'd spent at his joint," said June. "So I charged him $180 instead of the regular $150."

Miss Tegner, who's somewhat of a celebrity herself, pops up now and then in movie shorts on judo. A couple of Hollywood writers also are writing a book about her.

June said she got the idea of becoming a lady judo prof ten years ago while watching her lifeguard husband (she had two, but is single now) on a Chicago beach.

"I wanted to be strong, too," she said, "now look where I am!"

She studied judo in Chicago, and then taught there and in New York.

Miss Tegner once was giving an exhibition at a swank beach club in New Jersey when she spotted boxer Tommy Farr in the audience. She invited him to try a few holds on her. Farr paled and refused.

Tradition Now

"He was a broken-down movie director who hated Hollywood," she explained. "After a few weekly visits to my hill he disappeared. So I keep up the tradition."

Miss Tegner has a nine-year-old daughter, 80 pounds, who teaches a junior judo class and can easily throw her 17-year-old brother, 220 pounds.

"It's good, clean sport." Miss Tegner told us. "That hearse out in front doesn't mean a thing. I just happen to have an undertaker for a student."

Figure 20 Actor Groucho Marx poses with June Tegner (From the personal archives of Bruce Tegner)

Figure 21 From left to right, Teru Shimada, Jon Tegner, Humphrey Bogart, and June Tegner (From the personal archives of Bruce Tegner)

June Tegner was a proponent of women's self-defense and the author of numerous martial arts publications.

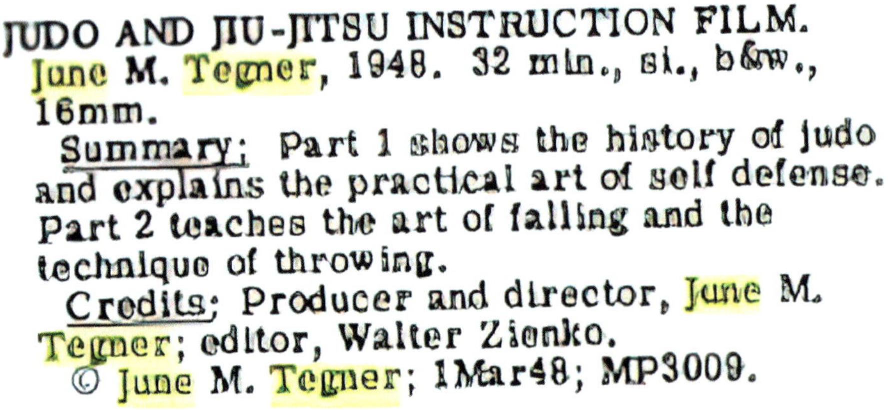

JUDO AND JIU-JITSU INSTRUCTION FILM.
June M. Tegner, 1948. 32 min., si., b&w.,
16mm.
  Summary: Part 1 shows the history of judo
and explains the practical art of self defense.
Part 2 teaches the art of falling and the
technique of throwing.
  Credits: Producer and director, June M.
Tegner; editor, Walter Zienko.
  © June M. Tegner; 1Mar48; MP3009.

Figure 22 An instructional film made by June Tegner listed on a catalog (Library of Congress)

Another Tegner family member, Carol, was also a student of Judo. Following in her parents' footsteps, she eventually pursued a career as a Judo instructor.

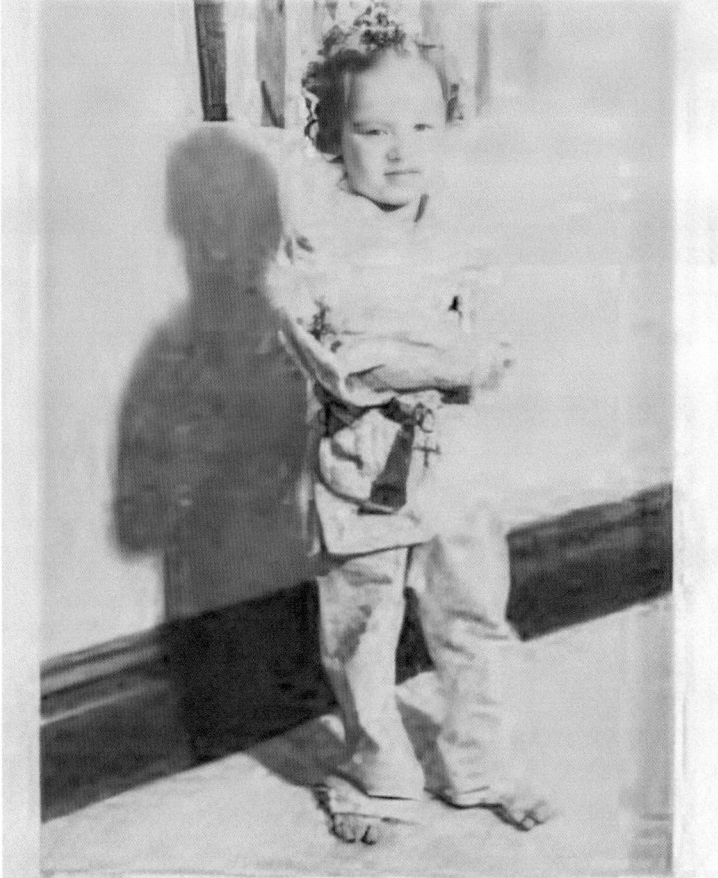

Carol Tegnér Receives Her Blue Belt Degree at the Age of Four. She Was the Youngest Child to Receive This Degree. "She's Lived Up To It."

Figure 23 A young Carol Tegner (Carvalho, Danilo)

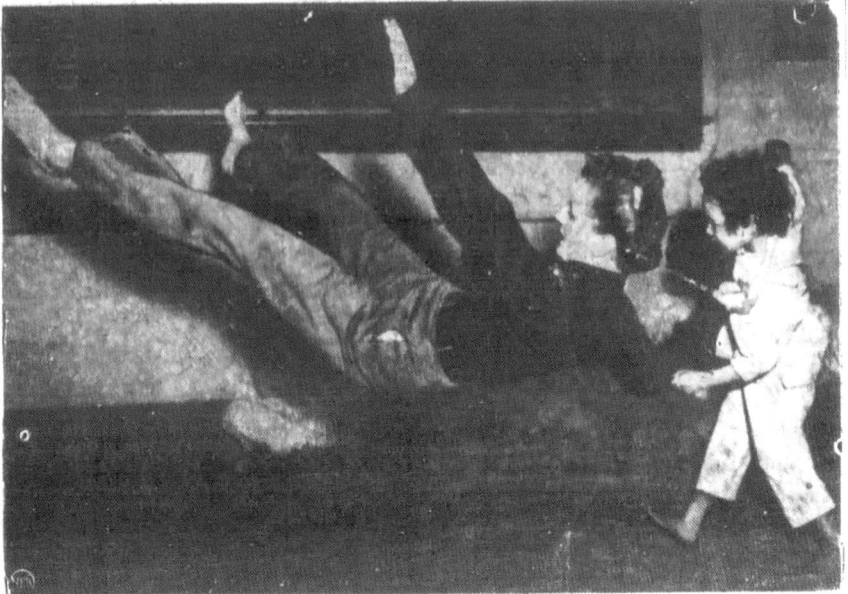

Oops, Mama!

Mrs. June Tegner decides there's something to this "judo" business as her 6-year-old daughter Carol sends her flying with a simple twist of the wrist during an exhibition at a Chicago judo club. War has increased Americans' interest in the study of this variation of ju-jitsu.

Figure 24 Little Carol Tegner throws her mother during a demonstration. Taken from "The Waterbury Democrat", February 15, 1943 (Library of Congress)

Figure 25 Carol demonstrates a strike to the solar plexus on her brother (From the personal archives of Bruce Tegner)

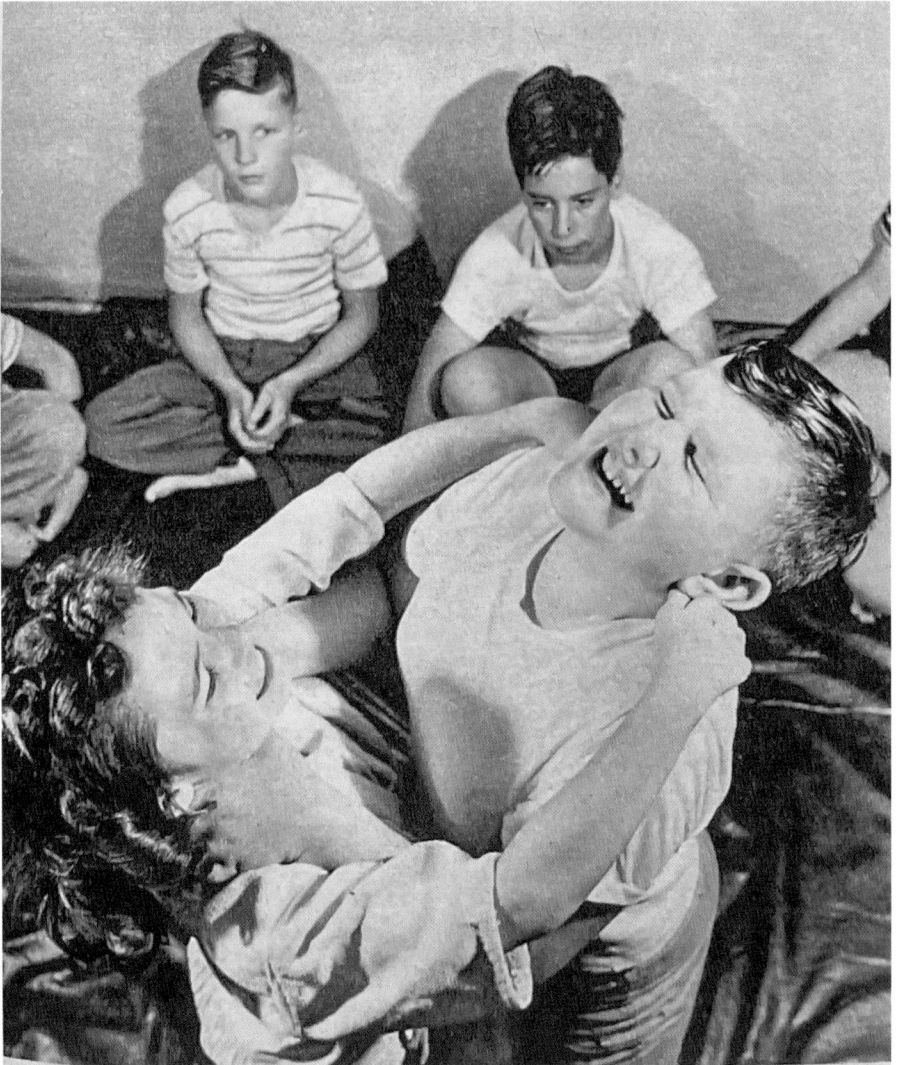

Figure 26 Carol demonstrates a strike to the vital points behind the ears, against a throat grab (From the personal archives of Bruce Tegner)

Figure 27 A young Carol demonstrates kuzushi (unbalancing an opponent) (From the personal archives of Bruce Tegner)

Figure 28 In the series of photos above, Carol demonstrates a defensive technique against a weapon attack (From the personal archives of Bruce Tegner)

Figure 29 Bruce being thrown over his sister's shoulder (From the personal archives of Bruce Tegner)

Figure 30 Carol Tegner performs a technique on fellow instructor James Widenot, dated July 17, 1956 (Adolph, Christine)

Figure 31 Carol blocks an attack initiated by her student, George Cruse (Adolph, Christine)

Figure 32 Carol performs a "Seoi Nage" on her student, Allen Smith (Adolph, Christine)

Figure 33 On June 8, 1956, Carol appeared as a guest on the famous show, "What's My Line? " (YouTube)

Figure 34 Carol and John Charles Daly (YouTube)

The young Bruce Tegner received instruction from his parents as well as Kuwashima. Tegner credits Kuwashima in one of his novels. Thus, it is reasonable to postulate that Kuwashima played a crucial part in shaping his life.

and to the memory of:
T. SHOZO KUWASHIMA,

my friend and teacher from early childhood. Of the many fine, high ranking instructors who were responsible for my training, Professor Kuwashima was most critical, most demanding, and most helpful. He gave many hours of many years to prepare me for Judo competition, and gave his most sincere encouragement to my decision to devote my life to a career of teaching.

Figure 35 Tegner's dedication to his former teacher (Tegner, Bruce)

In his parents' school, he began helping at the age of twelve, and by the time he was sixteen, he was a fully qualified teacher. He was the youngest second-degree black belt holder in American history at the time. Tegner received his second-degree black belt at the age of seventeen. According to several accounts, he won the 1949 California State Judo Championships. Later, he coached the army sport Judo teams and taught unarmed combat to members of the U.S. armed services in the early 1950s.

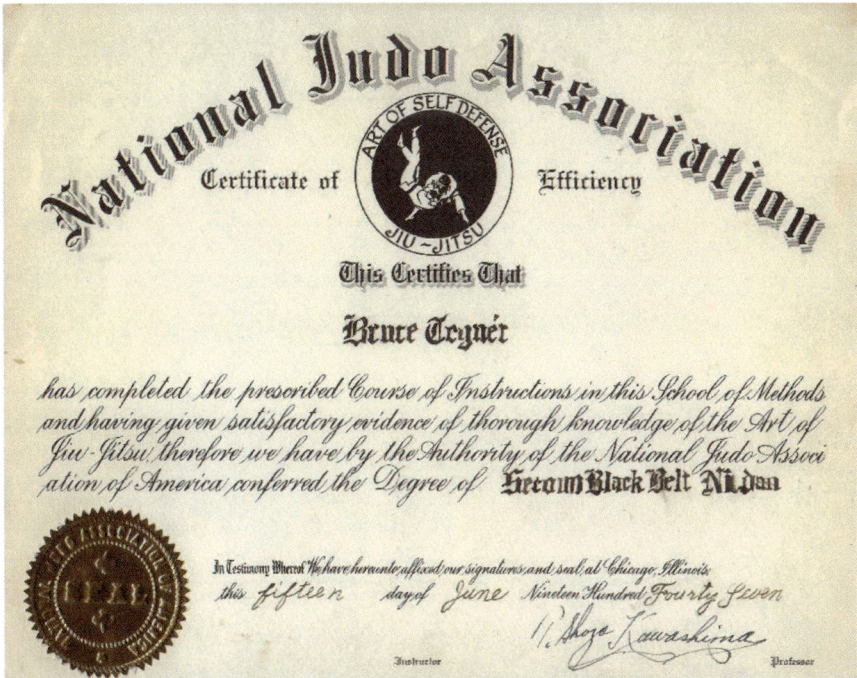

Figure 36 Bruce's black belt certificate, awarded by Shozo Kuwashima (From the personal archives of Bruce Tegner)

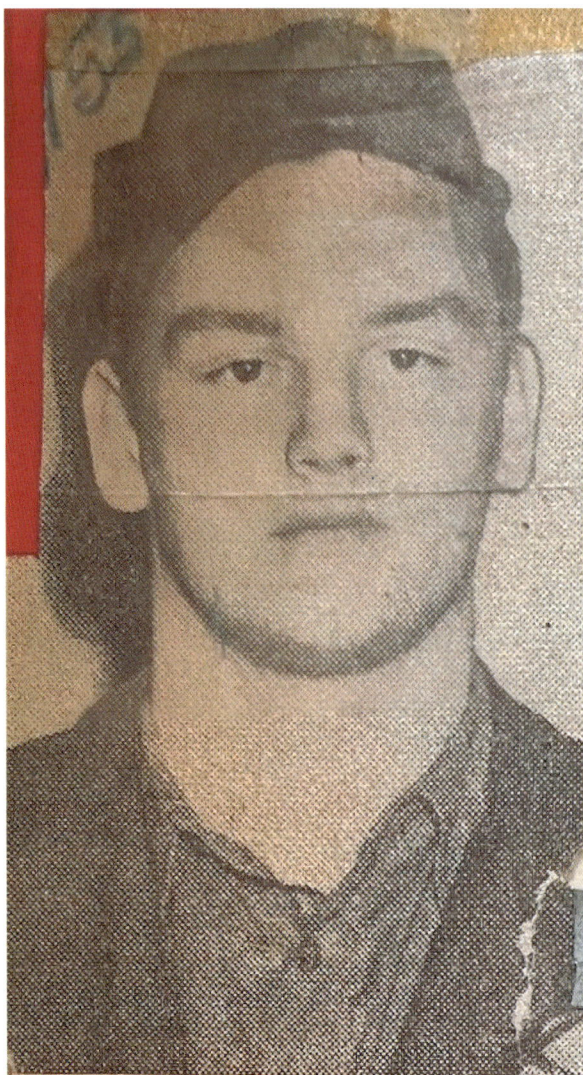

TWICE — Marine Reserve Pvt. Bruce Tegner gains high Judo honor second time.

Marine Wins Second Judo Expert Award

Pvt. Bruce Tegner, a member of the 2nd 105mm. Howitzer Battalion of the Los Angeles Organized Marine Corps Reserve, will be presented with his second black belt—highest distinction in the art of judo—at an exhibition to be held at the Naval and Marine Corps Reserve Armory, 850 Lilac Terrace, tomorrow at 8 p.m.

Pvt. Tegner, 17, is the youngest man in the United States to hold two black belts for his prowess in judo. The presentation of his second will follow an exhibition which is to feature many notables in the game.

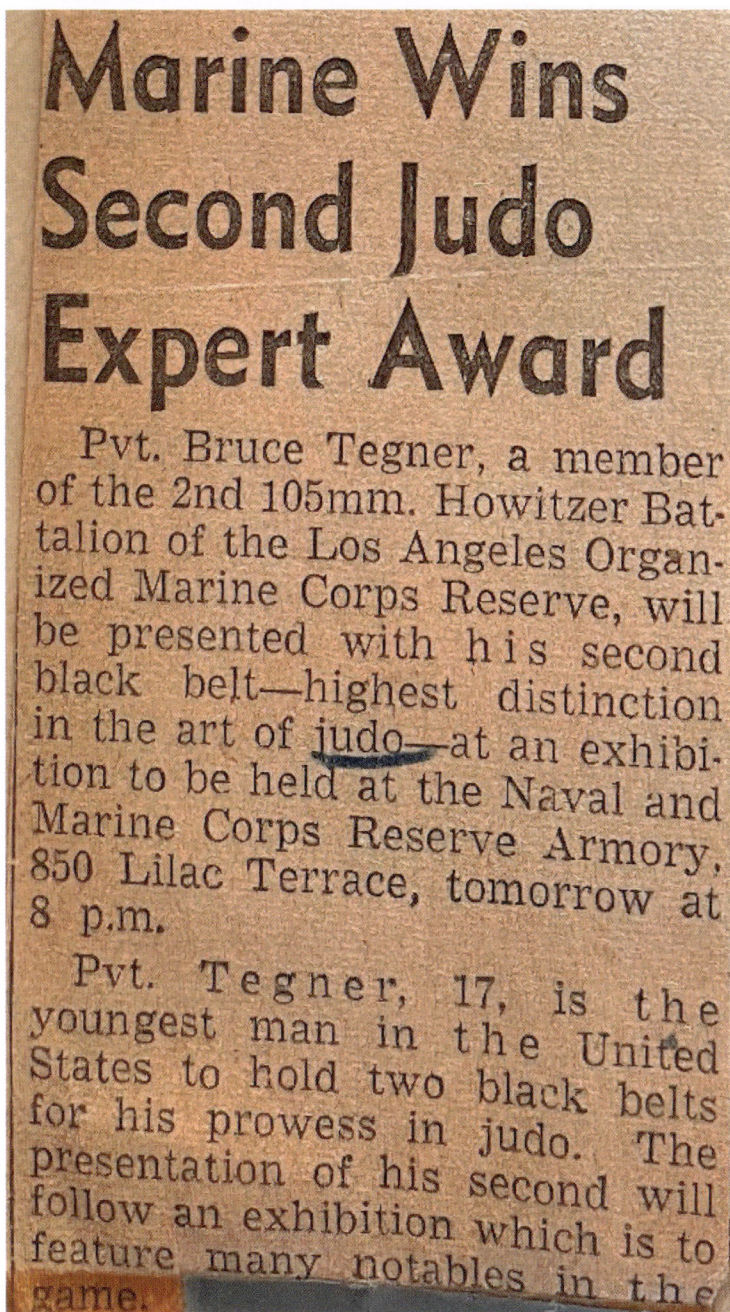

Figure 37 An article recognizing the status of Bruce's 2nd dan in Judo (From the personal archives of Bruce Tegner)

*Figure 38 Bruce Tegner (far right) at the Leaders Course in Camp Roberts, California
(From the personal archives of Bruce Tegner)*

I, Sergeant Bruce Tegner, request transfer to Provost Marshal General Center, Camp Gordon, Georgia, as Judo Instructor.

My experience and qualifications as a Judo Instructor are as follows:

My parents founded the National Judo Association at the time of my borth and my entire life has been spent in this Judo School. I started teaching at the age of fourteen and have taught hundreds of students, besides being head Judo Coach for teams in contests all over the United States. At the age of seventeen I received through contest, my "2nd Black Belt Degree" and was at that time youngest Occidental in the United States to have achieved this rank. I taught Judo to the 2nd Division 105 Howitzer Batallion, United States Marine Corp Reserve, from 1947 to 1949. From 1949 to 1950 I taught Judo to the National Guard, California. From 1950 to 1951, I taught Judo to the 40th M.P. Co., 40th Infantry Division, United States Army. Although I have specialized in Police and Military instructing, I have also worked with Judo on Radio, Television, and have done Technical Directing for the movie studios, have taught the American Federation of the Blind and beginners and post graduate work for Instructors, both in and out of the Armed Forces. I carry the authorization from the Kodo Kwan (Judo International Headquarters) Tokio, Japan, to judge and bestow Judo Degrees up to the First Black Belt Rank.

I feel that my qualifications would justify this transfer and would work for the betterment of the service.

Figure 39 Tegner's letter of request to be transferred to Camp Gordon and reassigned as a Judo Instructor (From the personal archives of Bruce Tegner)

12 March 1951

TO WHOM IT MAY CONCERN:

  Upon the request of Mr. and Mrs. John Tegner, the undersigned, during a visit to the Pentagon on official business, contacted the enlisted personnel branch of the Personnel Division of the Provost Marshal General's Office in an effort to determine if arrangements could be made to place Sergeant Bruce Tegner in an organization, in which his vast knowledge and experience in Judo could be utilized.

  The undersigned was informed by one Edward L. Turner, Administrative head of the Enlisted Personnel Section that Sgt. Tegner could be utilized to excellent advantage as Judo Instructor at the Provost Marshal General Center, Camp Gordon, Georgia. He stated that Judo instruction is an integral part of the curriculum at the Provost Marshal School. He further stated that the request for transfer must be originated by Sgt. Tegner and approved through channels to his office, at which time he would then issue the necessary instructions to have Sgt. Tegner transferred.

s/Harry E. Willard
t/HARRY E. WILLARD
 Lt Col USAF
 Exective Officer

Certified true copy

HOWARD D SHAVER
1st Lt Infantry

Figure 40 A letter approving the transfer of Tegner's Unit (From the personal archives of Bruce Tegner)

1 April 1952

SUBJECT: Letter of Commendation

TO: Sergeant Bruce Tegner
          The Leaders' Course
          87th Reconnaissance Battalion
          Camp Roberts, California

     1.   Upon the occasion of your release from my command
to return to civilian life, I wish to take this opportunity
to officially commend you for the services you have rendered.

     2.   During the period from 29 September 1951, to date,
your performance as an instructor of Unarmed Combat in the
Tactical Department has been outstanding.

     3.   The technical ability and the instructional ability
which you possess have been of great value, not only as an
instructor of students but also in the training of other
instructors. The conscientious and enthusiastic manner with
which you performed each duty, upholds the ideals of this
school. Your ability to understand the fundamentals of Judo
and to pass them on to others, greatly contributed to the
operation of this school and reflects credit upon yourself,
the Leaders' Course, and the military service of which you
are a member.

     4.   I wish to congratulate you on your successful
completion of this tour of active duty and would be gratified
to have you serve in my command again.

WAYNE F. DWYER
MAJOR   ARTY
Chief
Tactical Department

*Figure 41 A letter recognizing Tegner's achievements as an instructor in the marines
(From the personal archives of Bruce Tegner)*

Figure 42 A. B. Lee of the United States Naval Training Center in Bainbridge, performing a bayonet defense with his instructor, Bruce Tegner (Carvalho, Danilo)

Figure 43 Tegner (top), instructing bayonet techniques (Farkas, Emil)

2 LATER LIFE

CHAPTER AUTHORED BY ABDUL RASHID

After laying the groundwork in Judo, Bruce Tegner began studying other martial arts, including Karate, Savate, Aikido, and many others. It is unknown how long he studied these disciplines and what ranks he obtained. According to one report, he received an honorary 5th dan in Karate that was signed by Chojiro Tani.

book. A caption in English reads, "Certificate of Fifth Black Belt in Karate issued to Bruce Tegner by Shukokai (Japanese Karate Organization)." Actually, the certificate's Japanese words indicate, "An *honorary* fifth dan (fifth degree black belt) to Bruce Tegner on July 6, 1961" and the certificate was signed by Chojiro Tani.

Figure 44 An article on honorary grades, in which Tegner was mentioned. Taken from the Mar 1970 issue of Black Belt Magazine (Black Belt Magazine)

Figure 45 Chojiro Tani was born on 25 January 1921 in Kobe, Japan. He initially trained under Chojun Miyagi, the founder of Goju-Ryu, and eventually received his 2nd Dan. In 1939 he began karate training under the founder of Shito-Ryu, Kenwa Mabuni. Soon after, he established his own style, Tani-Ha Shito-Ryu (Facebook)

Figure 46 Tegner performing board breaking (Farkas, Emil)

After serving his country in the military, Bruce founded his own school in Hollywood around 1952, which he operated until 1967. It was during this period that he most likely formulated the theories for his system, JUKADO.

Figure 47 Bruce Tegner in his Hollywood dojo (Farkas, Emil)

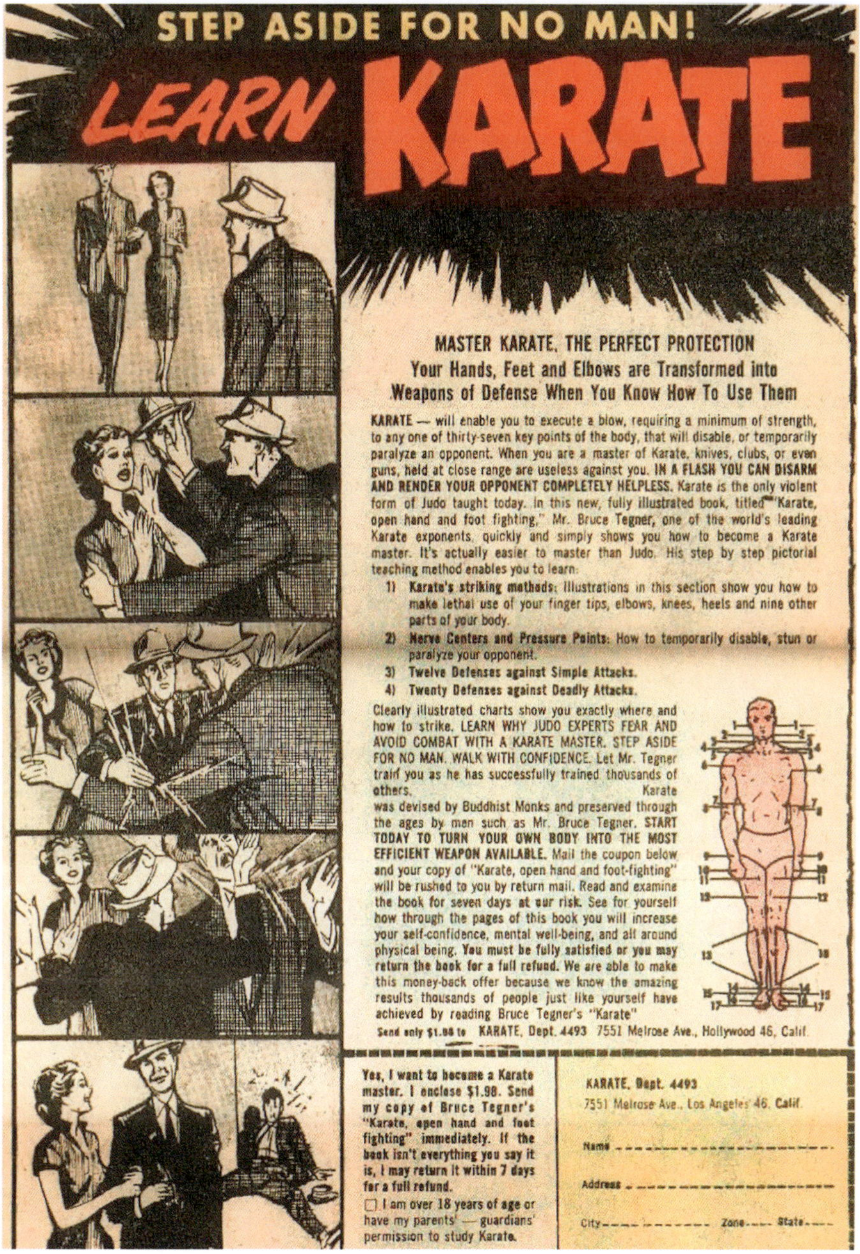

Figure 48 An advert promoting Tegner's book and school (YouTube)

Figure 49 Another advert where Tegner promotes the use of the "Yawara" as a self-defense tool (Ebay)

Figure 50 An advert for Tegner's school in Hollywood, California (From the personal archives of Bruce Tegner)

CLASS & PRIVATE LESSONS - DAY & EVENING INSTRUCTION

NATIONAL JUDO SCHOOLS
of Self Defense

ESTABLISHED 1928

CHILDREN & ADULTS - AGES 5 TO 55 YEARS

DICKENS 2-1985

FREE TEST LESSON

18655 VENTURA BLVD.
TARZANA, CALIFORNIA
(ACROSS FROM BROWN'S CENTER)

SELF DEFENSE   SPORT JUDO

NATIONAL JUDO SCHOOLS

- CHILDREN AND ADULTS, ALL AGES
- PRIVATE AND CLASS INSTRUCTION
- PROFESSIONAL INSTRUCTORS SINCE 1928
- PHYSICAL CONDITIONING, WEIGHT CONTROL

PHONE HOLLYWOOD 2-9222

BRUCE TEGNER   5544 SUNSET BLVD.
(1 BLK. W. OF WESTERN AVE.)   HOLLYWOOD 28, CALIF.

SELF-DEFENSE   SHERMAN OAKS
AND SPORT   14248 VENTURA BLVD.
                              ST 4-9226

NATIONAL JUDO SCHOOLS
CLASSES FOR CHILDREN AND ADULTS

HOLLYWOOD   PRESENTED BY
5544 SUNSET BLVD.
HO 2-9222

Figure 51 Business cards for the various schools Tegner owned (From the personal archives of Bruce Tegner)

56

Following in the footsteps of his mother, Bruce began writing books on various martial arts. The earliest publication Tegner authored would be "*The Open Hand and Foot Fighting*" which was released in 1960. Ironically, it was about Karate. He would publish numerous publications on the various systems over the decade that followed, making them widely known. Most readers could afford to purchase his books as they were reasonably priced, and many of his writings were translated into various languages.

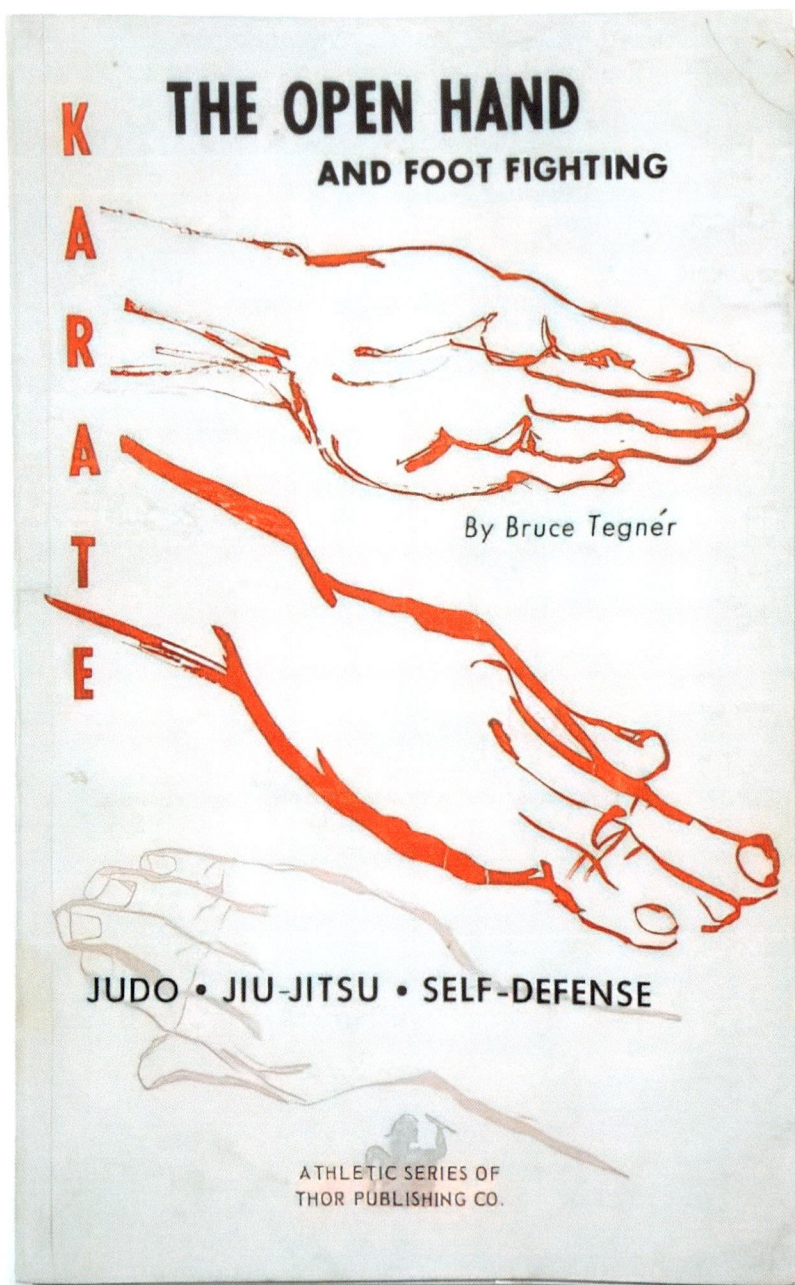

Figure 52 Pictured above is Bruce Lee's personal copy of Tegner's first book (Julien's Auctions)

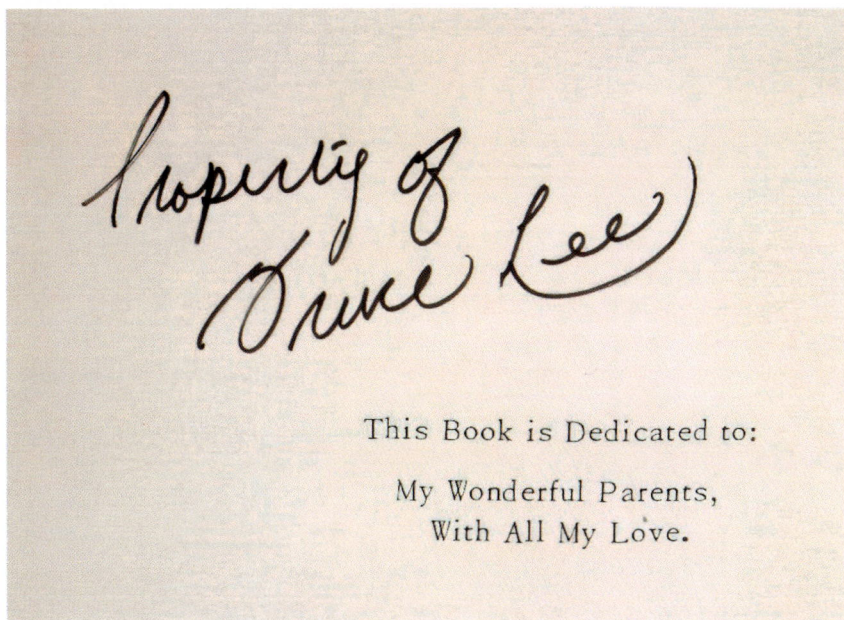

Property of
Bruce Lee

This Book is Dedicated to:

My Wonderful Parents,
With All My Love.

Figure 53 Bruce Lee's signed copy of the book (Julien's Auctions)

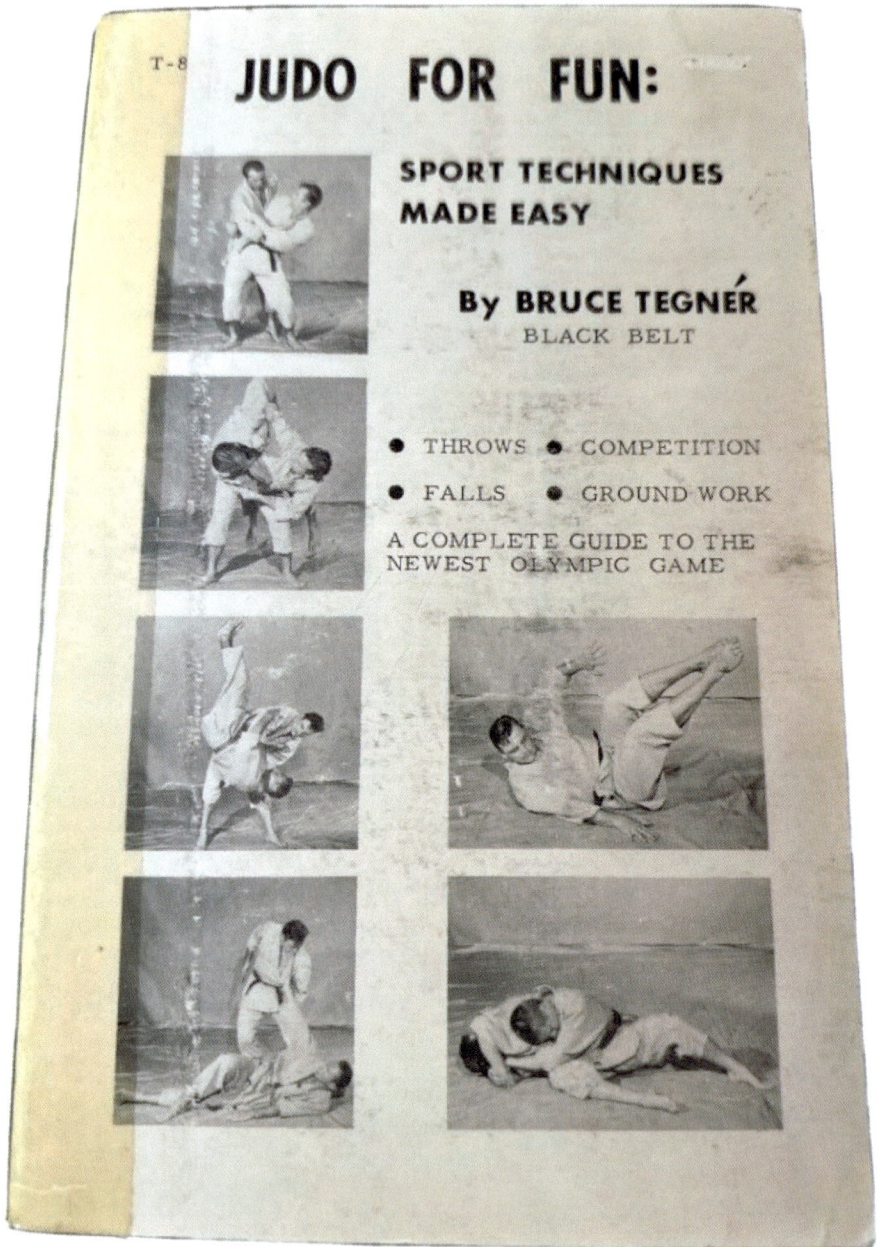

Figure 54 Another Tegner book, released in 1961 (eBay)

AIKIDO SELF-DEFENSE:

Holds & Locks for Modern Use

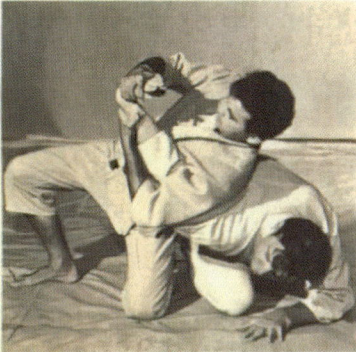

By BRUCE TEGNER

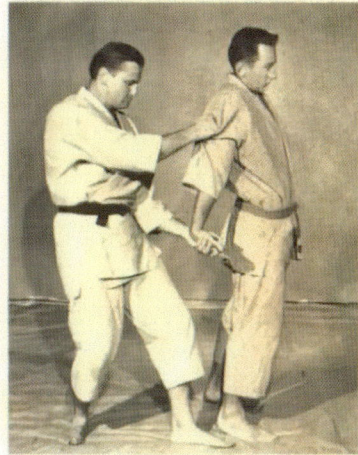

Aikido is the fascinating Art of self-defense which uses arm locks, body locks, leg locks and a great many holds and throws. It is ideal for those who wish to know a means of protection without the use of harsh or violent actions. It teaches and develops a calm mental attitude as part of the training.

Figure 55 A book which he authored on Aikido (Facebook)

Figure 56 Another one on Savate, which was published in 1970 (Amazon)

LIBRO COMPLETO DE

KARATE

Un curso ilustrado de karate deportivo,
de principiante a cinta negra.

UNIVERSO

BRUCE TEGNER

Figure 57 Tegner's Karate book translated into Spanish (Archive)

On April 5, 1977, he married the well-known social activist Alice McGrath, who helped him with the preparation of the manuscripts and the publication of his books. Their marriage was short-lived, but they lived together as a couple beginning in 1959 until Bruce's death.

Figure 58 Born in 1917, Alice Greenfield McGrath was an American activist best known for her involvement in the 1942 case of the "Sleepy Lagoon Murder". She also trained in martial arts and held a brown belt in Judo (From the personal archives of Bruce Tegner)

Figure 59 Bruce Tegner met Alice McGrath around 1958 when Alice brought her son to Bruce's judo studio to learn self-defense. By 1959, Bruce and Alice were living together as partners and working as a team to publish Bruce's books on martial arts (From the personal archives of Bruce Tegner)

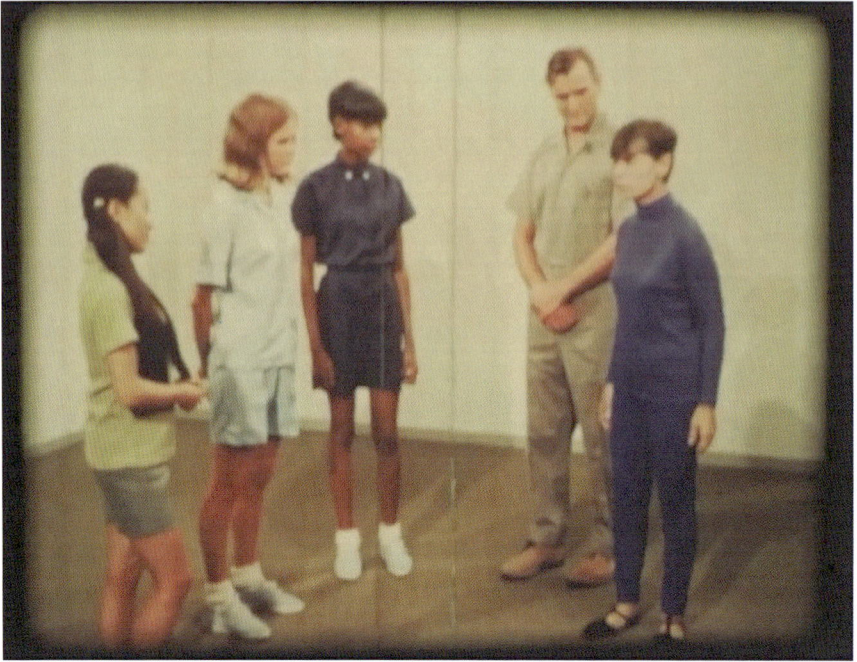

Figure 60 Alice and Bruce conducting a self-defense class for girls (YouTube)

Ricky Nelson, Joan Crawford, George Reeves, and James Coburn were among the Hollywood stars who received instruction from Tegner. In several films, namely *"The Manchurian Candidate,"* starring Henry Silva and Frank Sinatra, he also acted as a fight choreographer and advisor.

Figure 61 Joan Crawford (left), on the set of 'The Caretakers' with Bruce Tegner and co-star Constance Ford (Joan Crawford Best)

Figure 62 Tegner demonstrates a technique to Crawford (Joan Crawford Best)

Figure 63 Gloria Talbott and Tegner, during the shooting of "Girls Town" (EMovie Poster)

Figure 64 Tegner (left) along with James Coburn in "Our Man Flint", which was released in 1966 (YouTube)

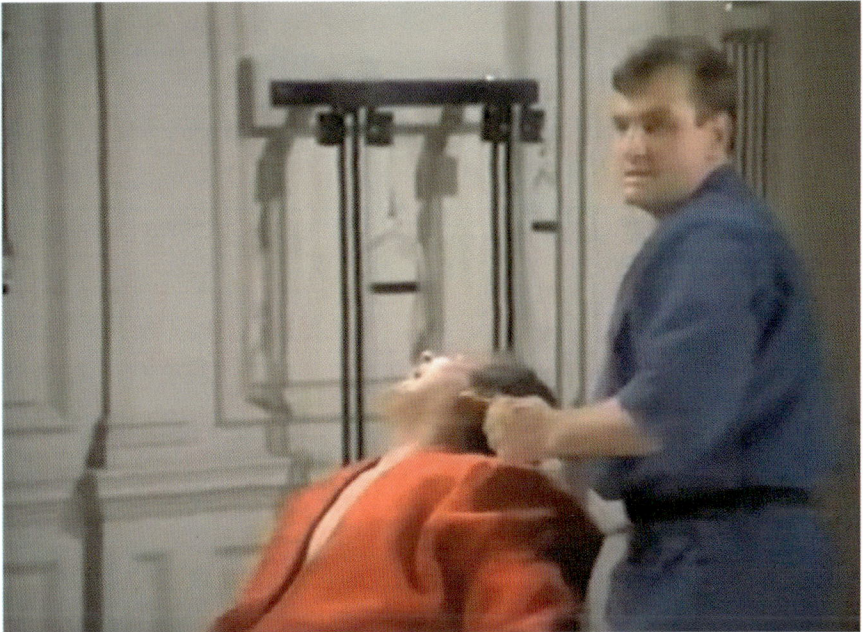

Figure 65 Tegner demonstrates martial arts in the 1967 movie, "Good Times", starring Sonny & Cher (YouTube)

Figure 66 A signed photograph from George Reeves to the Tegners (From the personal archives of Bruce Tegner)

On January 8, 1960, Tegner demonstrated tameshiwari (*brick breaking*) on the television show "*The Detectives*", presenting Karate to the American audience for the very first time.

Figure 67 Tegner preparing to demonstrate "tameshiwari " in an episode on "The Detectives", along with Robert Taylor to his far right (YouTube)

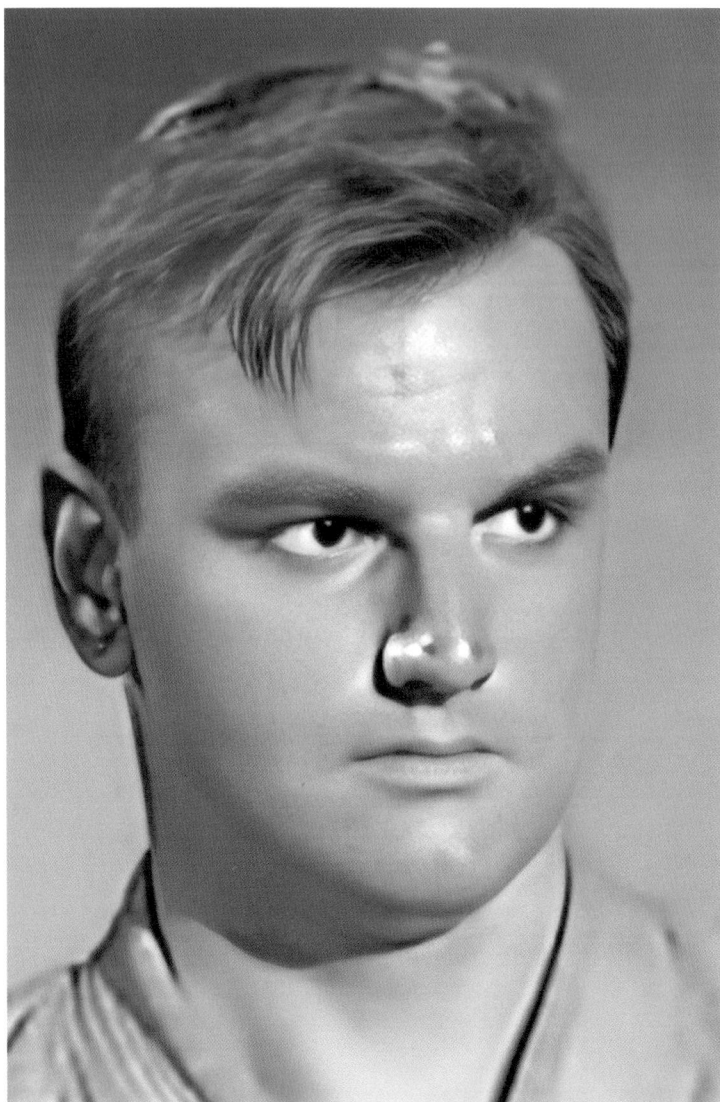

Figure 68 Though Tegner's screen time was less than 5 minutes, he made a prominent impact on the audience with his performance (YouTube)

On the television program *"The Adventures of Ozzie and Harriet,"* Tegner would give another Karate demonstration a year later. Ricky Nelson, one of his students, was accompanying him. The "boom" of karate was caused by the presence of such a prominent celebrity practicing the art.

Figure 69 Singer, Ricky Nelson performing a "Jodan age uke" (upward block) with Tegner (Farkas, Emil)

Ed Parker, another well-known name in American martial arts, held Tegner in high regard because of his Karate demonstrations. He claimed that many pupils entered his dojos in Pasadena and Santa Monica carrying a Tegner-authored Karate book.

Figure 70 Parker was born in Hawaii and started training in Judo and Boxing at an early age. During the 1940s, he started training in Kenpō under William Chow. Eventually, he developed his own style "American Kenpo" which he felt would be applicable to the streets of America. In his later years, he acted as Elvis Presley's bodyguard. Parker is best known for his creative business mindset, through which he helped other martial artists establish themselves. (Facebook)

The Karate performances of Tegner inspired Hollywood actor Rick Jason to train in the martial arts, which he began doing so with Parker. In the 1961 television series *"The Case of the Dangerous Robin,"* Jason utilized his Karate *"abilities"* to get out of tricky predicaments.

Figure 71 A poster for the series, which ran from October 1960 to July 1961 (Ctva)

Tegner's promotion of Karate led to Parker later inviting him to his martial arts event, "*The Long Beach Tournament*," which was held in August 1964. Tegner's invitation was contentious since many believed he had not significantly contributed to the growth of martial arts. Parker, on the other hand, disagreed, as seen in a 1990 interview with him.

And although some objected to my inviting Bruce Tegner, I reminded them that Tegner's books did influence many to take up the martial arts.

Figure 72 An interview with Parker, taken from the Dec 1990 issue of Black Belt Magazine (Black Belt Magazine)

Bruce Lee's debut of his legendary one-inch punch and two-finger push-ups occurred during this tournament. These performances eventually led to his fame.

Figure 73 A poster for the International Karate Championships, held in Los Angeles, 1964 (PBA Galleries)

Figure 74 Lee demonstrating his famous one-inch punch (Raymond, Charles)

Figure 75 Parker and Lee sometime in 1964 (YouTube)

3 LEGACY

CHAPTER AUTHORED BY GEORGE REGO

While individuals such as the prominent movie star Bruce Lee are often credited with being the first modern martial artist to "think outside the box" with the advocacy of martial artists not being dogmatically tied down by any one particular style, a careful reading of history demonstrates that Lee was by no means the first. Bruce Tegner is a prominent American martial artist who was advocating cross-pollination before famous individuals, including Bruce Lee, were even studying martial arts at all, or were even born. Ironically, a few decades later, Lee would teach in the area of Hollywood, California, where Tegner had established himself.

Figure 76 Lee and his student, Coburn (Twitter)

Figure 77 Lee working with Sharon Tate on the set of "The Wrecking Crew" (Loi, Lak)

While Tegner's background and core as a martial artist was inextricably linked to the art of jujutsu, or old-school judo, he was quite open and well-versed in several other fighting methods. Even within the scope of judo, he was quite progressive in his thinking and not afraid to critique the common philosophical tropes or pedagogical methods associated with it. Drawing from his own words in his book titled *Bruce Tegner's Complete Book of Judo*, one can read several progressive and challenging statements that most judoka of today would not feel comfortable making... to say nothing of making these statements in the era in which he did make them. Whether one agrees in full, in part, or not at all with his statements is up to the individual reader. Nonetheless, what is quite obvious is that Tegner was willing to challenge the status quo and many conventional ideas.

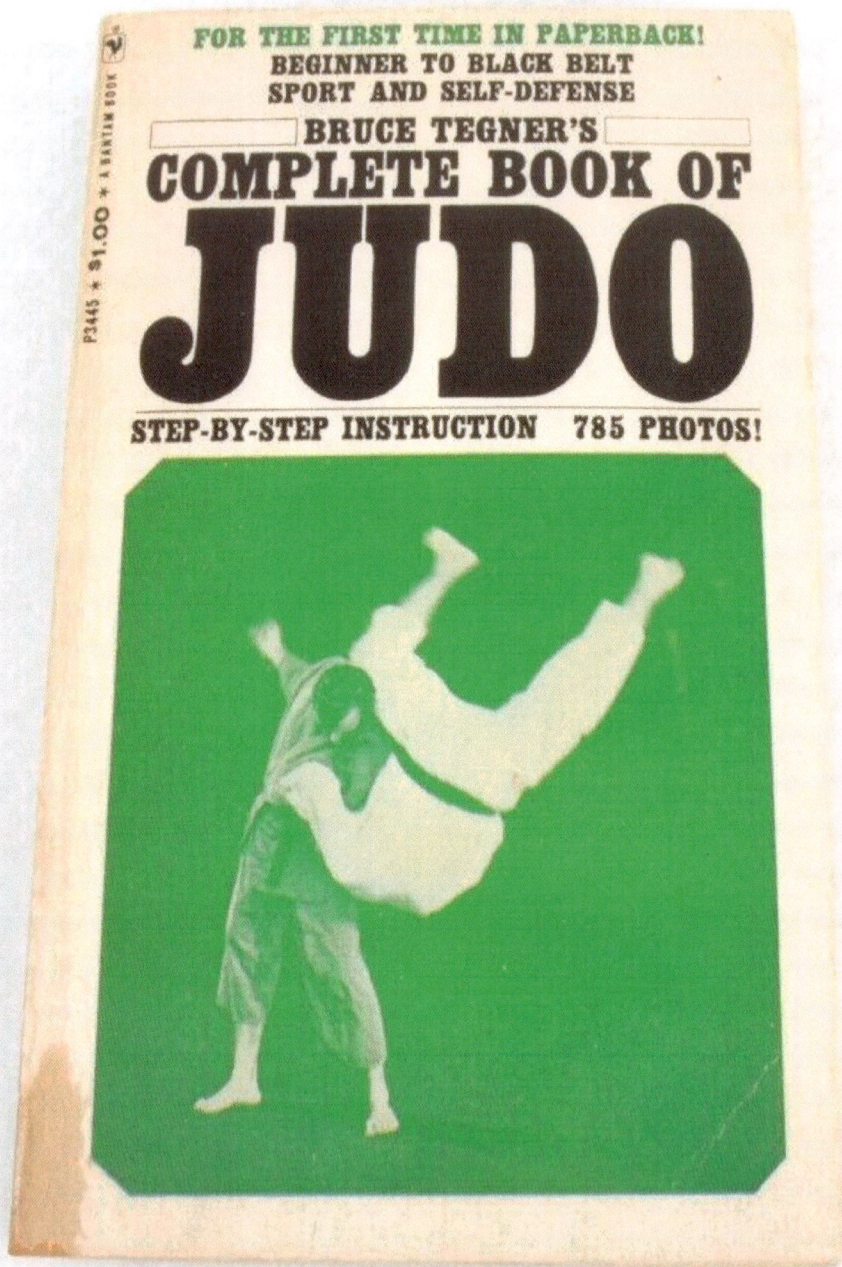

Figure 78 One of Tegner's critically acclaimed books (eBay)

For example, Tegner challenges the notion that Judo is a way of life. He states on page 11 of the above-mentioned book:

"There is a popular misconception which implies that Judo must be approached with an almost religious reverence. It is said that Judo is not merely a physical activity; it is a Way of Life. If you ask a modern proponent of the Way of Life notion what he means by that phrase, two related ideas develop: (1) That you must devote your entire life to the study of Judo, making it your central activity; (2) That through the serious study of Judo you will mysteriously and automatically become a more spiritual, highly moral person. Neither of these explanations has validity..."

While most martial artists view the notion of "DO" (道) or "The Way " as a philosophical means that broadens the purpose and reach of the combative arts, Tegner believed that overstating this was actually detrimental to the martial arts. A notion that was as unique then as it is now. In the same Judo text noted above, he expands on this idea:

"Modern proponents of Judo as a Way of Life make a mistake when they assume that 'devotion to the art,' to use their phrase, is the only way to a physical and mental harmony which could lead to a better, more useful, more reasonable and more pleasurable life. Dr. Kano's concept of the most efficient use of mental and physical

energy for the accomplishment of a definitive purpose is not the exclusive property of Judo or Judo players. To make such a claim is not in the interest of promoting Judo play... Judo is wonderful, but it is not The Only Way...

To propose Judo as a Way of Life is to limit its acceptance. However, we can strongly recommend the practice of Judo on the basis of demonstrable benefits, which have usefulness in modern life; Judo is splendid exercise, and, unlike many exercises, it is great fun to do. Judo is marvelous for mind-body coordination; it is a participation rather than a spectator activity; and it is possible, if you have the desire, to improve all other activities of your life if you will apply what you have learned in Judo practice.

In this mechanized American era, we desperately need to encourage great numbers of people to participate in physical activity. We are a nation of watchers, and we cannot continue this trend without impoverishing our mental and physical health. The idea of Judo, it seems to me, is particularly appropriate for Americans... Judo need not be thought of as a Way of Life, but it can be a marvelous way to enrich your life.

And what about the notion that Judo, to be studied seriously, must be the central activity of your life? This is sheer nonsense. If the only people allowed to practice Judo were those who had the time and inclination to make it the most important activity of their lives, we would have only a tiny number of Judo players in the entire country. Obviously, the amount of time you spend at Judo must be determined by many factors — the responsibility you have to your schoolwork, your job, your family, and the like.

The purpose for which you are studying Judo will also determine the amount of time you will want to spend at it: if your aim is to engage in an enjoyable, healthful few hours of exercise each week, you want to become a champion Judo tournament player then it will certainly have to be your primary activity. And there are degrees of involvement between these two extremes; yours is the job of deciding the amount and degree of your commitment. There is nothing in Dr. Kano's presentation of Judo to indicate otherwise.``

We can see here that in an era that was quite prone to the near "religiofication" of the martial arts by overzealous westerners, Tegner was keen to emphasize that one should place the study of martial arts in its proper context... and that context could and would be different based on individual objectives. To be clear, Tegner fully dedicated his life to the martial arts. Further, he was not opposed to anyone else doing the same. It is a safe bet to assume he would support such a noble endeavor. However, his central point is that one didn't need to make martial arts a full-blown "Way of Life" in order to draw life-enhancing benefits from them. Tegner strongly believed that if martial arts were presented to prospective students as an ultimatum, "Either make the art your 'Way of Life" or don't practice at all," many fewer people would be drawn to them.

As he points out in his writings, one could easily dedicate their life to the sport of Tennis or Swimming by making it the central focal point of their lives. However, many others can take a much more modest approach to those activities and still draw enormous benefit. If one is made to believe that in order to take up Swimming or Tennis it necessitates making that activity their "Way of Life," then the art would be of value to a tiny group of people.

Figure 79 Tegner demonstrating a jump front kick (From the personal archives of Bruce Tegner)

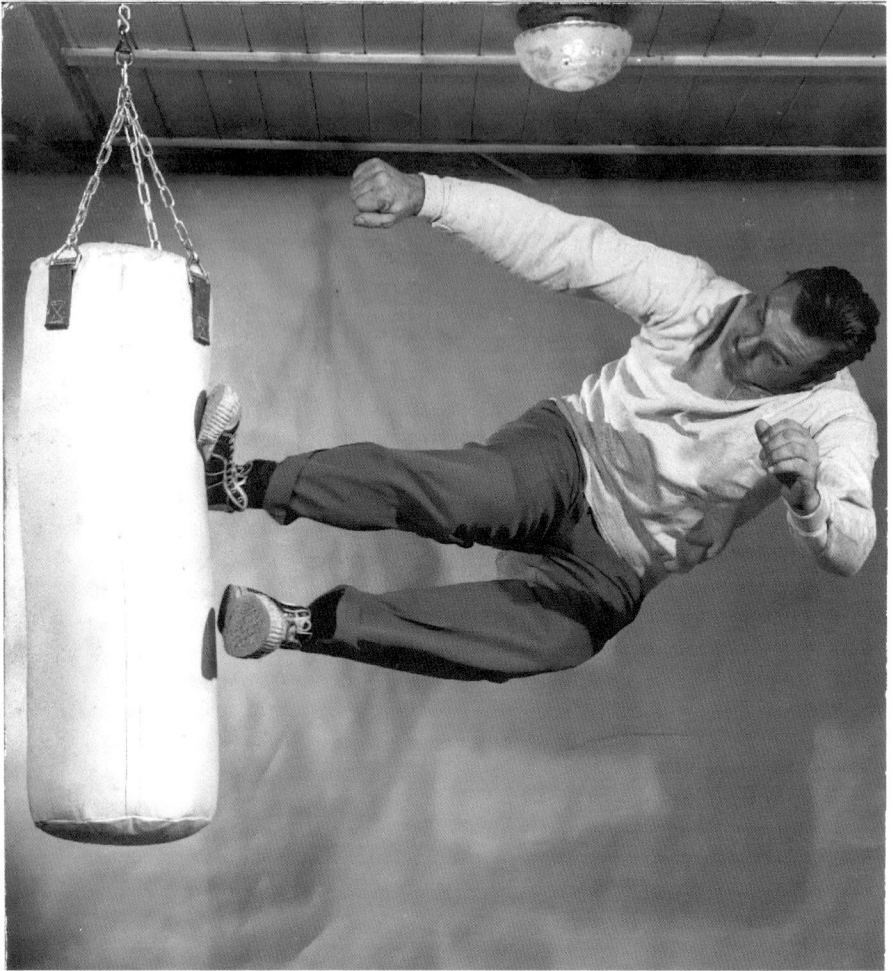

Figure 80 Tegner demonstrating a jump side kick (From the personal archives of Bruce Tegner)

Figure 81 Tegner and fellow Judoka, Anton Geesink (From the personal archives of Bruce Tegner)

While Jigoro Kano, the founder of Kodokan Judo, had some of the loftiest possible goals one could imagine for the art of Judo, Tegner did not see his views in any way conflicting with Master Kano. While this might seem obvious to most readers now, in Tegner's time, he was one of the very few voices who were cutting against the grain by both advocating for the wide dissemination of martial arts while also trying to ensure that the various arts didn't inadvertently get in their own way by alienating the very people that could benefit most from them.

From a technical and educational perspective, Tegner held views that could be controversial in most Judo circles today and were absolutely not common in his own time. Whether one agrees or disagrees, he was courageous in not shying away from stating views boldly. He stated:

"Dr. Kano made drastic changes in the forms of the ancient Jitsus (sic) to suit the needs of his time; the acceptance of change is inherent in his method. Everything about his approach encourages us to make changes as they are required. Dr. Kano gave leadership with his original and inventive thinking, but his followers have institutionalized his originality and want to make further originality a heresy."

There are several examples of Tegner's openness to change and innovation in Judo. For one, he was an advocate for using native languages for the naming of Judo techniques. He was not a proponent of Japanese being used as the universal language of Judo. Clearly, he was in the minority opinion here but not entirely alone. Perhaps more dramatic was his view on Judo kata. Tegner dedicates a large section of his *"Complete Book of Judo"* to Judo kata. He advocates the preservation of traditional Kodokan kata and outlines them in great detail, which was uncommon even in most Japanese Judo texts of the time or today. Tegner also includes old-style Judo kata that are no longer officially recognized by the Kodokan, such as Go no Sen no Kata.

Figure 82 Tegner executes a throw on his student (Farkas, Emil)

However, what is of particular note is his strong presentation for "new style" kata. He even encourages advanced students to develop their own kata. He outlines this in detail by stating the following:

"Times have changed! There is nothing sacred about the forms of Judo. They were invented by Japanese humans, and it should not be cause for shock than an American human has devised a new set of forms for modern practice. While Old-Style forms are beautiful and quaint, we should remember that they were not intended to be quaint, they have become quaint with the passing of time. The forms of sword attack and forms of kneeling attack, for instance, were based on very ordinary situations of that time. The Japanese did carry swords and daggers; they did kneel instead of sitting on chairs. So, to invent forms which included these situations was a very natural development for that culture.

`Moreover, the defense in the Old-Style forms was limited and determined by the culture in which they occurred. Grabbing and grappling with a dagger-wielding arm is not a good defense; from a kneeling position it might be the only possible defense. When performing the Old-Style forms, you should not be concerned with the practicality of the techniques, but only with performing them with style and grace.

I have now added some forms which are more appropriate to our time. Though you should not imagine that learning forms is the way of becoming completely proficient in street defense, at least, with these new forms, you are becoming familiar with movements and actions which have some resemblance to useful methods of street defense.

Students should be encouraged to invent additional forms. It is excellent, creative Judo practice to develop forms and demonstrate them. For the students who have no interest in contests and have completed the required Old-Style forms for degree advancement, the encouragement of personal creativity is a way of assuring their continuing interest in Judo. Formula learning develops only one part of the student; creativity develops a more interesting, lively, participating human being."

Figure 83 Tegner demonstrating a jumping knee strike (From the personal archives of Bruce Tegner)

Tegner was also cutting against the grain with his approach to martial arts practice outside of Judo. Tegner's personal and educational approach is epitomized by the philosophy summarized by Bruce Lee a few decades later: "*Absorb what is useful. Discard what is not. Add what is uniquely your own.*" Tegner was a bit of a ronin – a masterless warrior – in the American martial arts landscape. He didn't attach himself too tightly to any particular group or style and yet he was well acquainted with a wide variety of martial arts. His core was always Judo and Jujutsu. His later work focused on a personal self-defense system he devised that he called JUKADO.

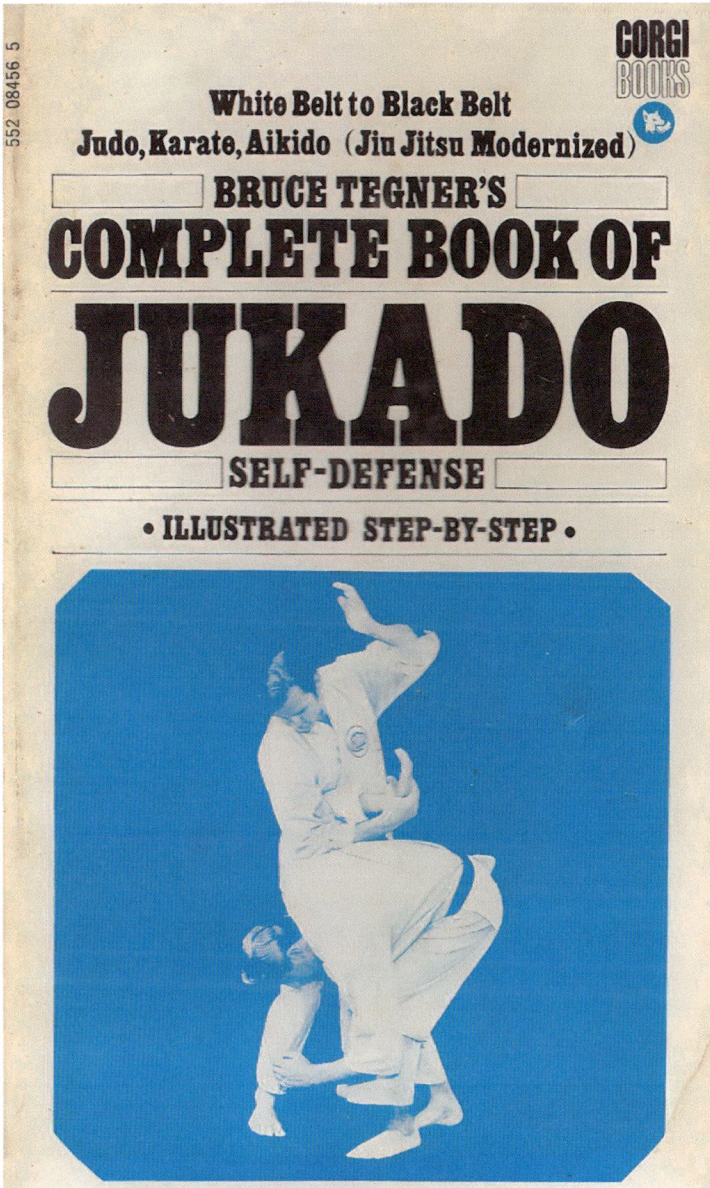

Figure 84 The first edition of Tegner's book on "Jukado" (Amazon)

Figure 85 Tegner dealing with multiple attackers (From the personal archives of Bruce Tegner)

To say that Bruce Tegner was prolific is a massive understatement. His reference books went an immensely long way in exposing the masses to a variety of martial arts from both Asia and Europe. Many of his ideas were popular. Others were controversial. Tegner definitely had plenty of critics. Many experienced martial artists of the time interpreted his publication of such a wide variety of texts on so many distinct martial arts as a claim that he was a high-level expert in all of them.

Whether Tegner thought of himself as such or was simply trying to "get the word out" is a judgment call that each individual can make. What is definitely beyond debate is that Tegner was a man who dedicated his life to martial arts proliferation and did so in a way that wasn't conventional for the time. He was anything but a cookie-cutter and wasn't overly concerned with the validation of those in central authority positions. He explored a wide variety of martial arts, challenged many "sacred cow" ideas, and was always quite forward thinking. The early martial arts seen in America and beyond, through his books, was greatly influenced by his considerable contributions. Unquestionably, Tegner was a pioneer who left his permanent mark on the world of martial arts.

4 INTERVIEW WITH BOB ROSENBAUM

CHAPTER AUTHORED BY ABDUL RASHID

Notes from interview with the late Bob Rosenbaum on 4/30/23. By Holly Woolson

Figure 86 Portrait of the late Bob Rosenbaum (Self Defense Trivandrum)

Bob trained with Bruce beginning in June of 1959 until October of 1968 when Joel Bracey became a head instructor. Bruce sold the studio around 1969. Bob was 15 years old when he first came to Bruce's studio to study martial arts. He remembers being in the same class as Alice's son Dan. Dan was younger than Bob. When Dad was about 9 years old, he threw Bob down during a class workout. This really surprised Bob since Dan was so much younger and smaller than Bob.

Bruce eventually owned two schools that were strictly his – that he ran on his own without his parents (June and Jon Tegner). They sold him at least one of these studios and then went on to open another, possibly in Glendale:

1. 5544 Sunset Blvd., Los Angeles

2. 59 Sunset Blvd., Los Angeles

Bruce's favorite form of martial art was Judo. He preferred first Judo, then Karate, and third Jujitsu. Bruce combined the forms of Judo and Karate into what he called "Jukado." Bruce didn't practice Aikido or Kung Fu. He wrote these books with ghost writers. Bruce taught and wrote books because he wanted to share something that he loved. Alice was the reason Bruce wrote books. She would write the text while Bruce created the content and took the photographs.

But Bruce would have been happy just to teach. Bruce loved to teach. Although Bruce wrote a book on Karate, he was not a "karate man." He knew enough to understand it. Bruce's philosophy about martial arts was this: the most important weapon is the mind. His teaching was not about fighting. Every class was half about the art, and half about self-defense, which he saw as totally separate and had nothing to do with the martial art. He had a different goal than many other teachers of martial arts. Bruce took the sport and the art into more of a reality-based mentality. A practical approach.

Bruce always valued education and encouraged Bob to pursue more education. Bruce himself went back to community college two semesters a year, seeing a connection between athletic and intellectual development. He said to never stop growing the mind.

Bob remembers when James Coburn was one of Bruce's students. He did a movie called "Big Hercules." He also remembers a Life Magazine photo shoot of the kids at Tegner's studio. After Bruce retired, Bob studied with Joe Lewis who was a physical fighter. Bruce was a father figure to Bob. At the end of the interview, Bob said that if he had ever done anything good in his life, it was because of Bruce Tegner.

5 TIMELINE OF TENGER'S LIFE

CHAPTER AUTHORED BY ABDUL RASHID

Timeline of Bruce Tegner's life

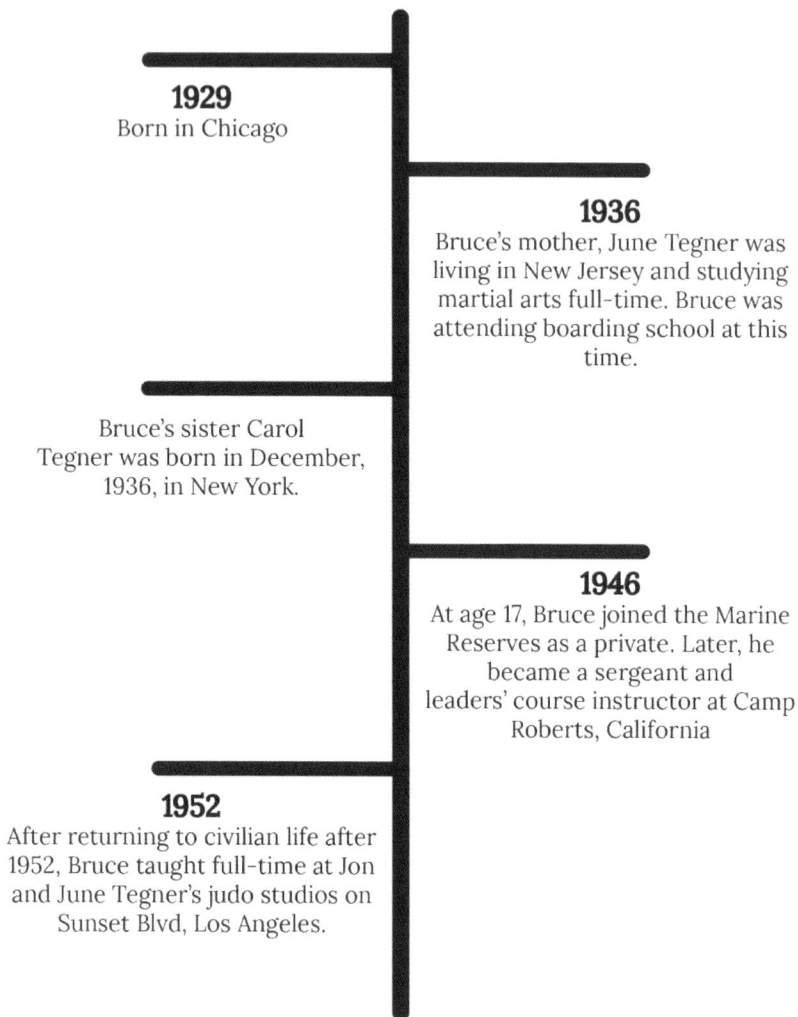

1929
Born in Chicago

1936
Bruce's mother, June Tegner was living in New Jersey and studying martial arts full-time. Bruce was attending boarding school at this time.

Bruce's sister Carol Tegner was born in December, 1936, in New York.

1946
At age 17, Bruce joined the Marine Reserves as a private. Later, he became a sergeant and leaders' course instructor at Camp Roberts, California

1952
After returning to civilian life after 1952, Bruce taught full-time at Jon and June Tegner's judo studios on Sunset Blvd, Los Angeles.

1958

Alice McGrath brought her son Dan to study with Bruce because Dan was being bullied at school.

1959

Bruce and Alice began living together. Alice collaborated on his books from 1959 on. All of the writing was done by her. Bruce would explain the moves and she would write down the descriptions.

1965

Bruce and Alice move to Ventura, California.

1969

Bruce sold his studio in Los Angeles and retired from teaching martial arts, but continued to publish books with Alice.

1970s

Bruce took up backpacking and began teaching outdoor survival at Ventura College.

1983
Bruce and Alice published The Survival Book: The Complete Handbook of Survival Techniques and First Aid for Natural and Man-made Disasters and Emergencies.

1985
On August 28, 1985, Bruce died of a heart attack in Ventura. His ashes were scattered at sea near the Ventura Harbor where he loved to sail.

This page is intentionally left blank.

ABOUT THE AUTHORS

Abdul Rashid

I started training in the martial arts sometime in 2012. My journey began with Aikido. Progressively, I gained an immense interest in the martial arts. Particularly, the Japanese martial arts. Overtime, I switched to Karate for a brief period, before starting with Jujitsu and boxing. As a past time, I enjoy researching about the martial arts and writing articles about them. I will always be a student of the arts, longing to seek knowledge.

George Rego

George Rego is a Portuguese-American lifelong martial artist. He is also the author of the best selling book, The Founding of Jujutsu & Judo in America. Today he is widely recognized as one of the most prominent masters, teachers, and practitioners in the martial art of Jukido Jujitsu. He is a direct student of American martial arts pioneer, Master Paul Arel.

From youngsters with special needs to members of the military special forces, Rego has trained people from all walks of life. He firmly believes in the ability of genuine martial arts for self-defense and striving for personal perfection.

While his teaching focuses exclusively on martial arts for realistic self-defense, Rego has competed successfully —including winning the 2015 AAU National Freestyle Judo Championship (Lightweight Masters).

The Jukido Academy is owned and run by Rego and is located in Palm Coast, Florida. His work may be found on YouTube and other social media, all of which are accessible through the main website of his dojo, www.floridajukido.com.

Please feel free to look through the following pages and purchase our other titles if interested. Available on Amazon

The Founding of Jujutsu & Judo in America

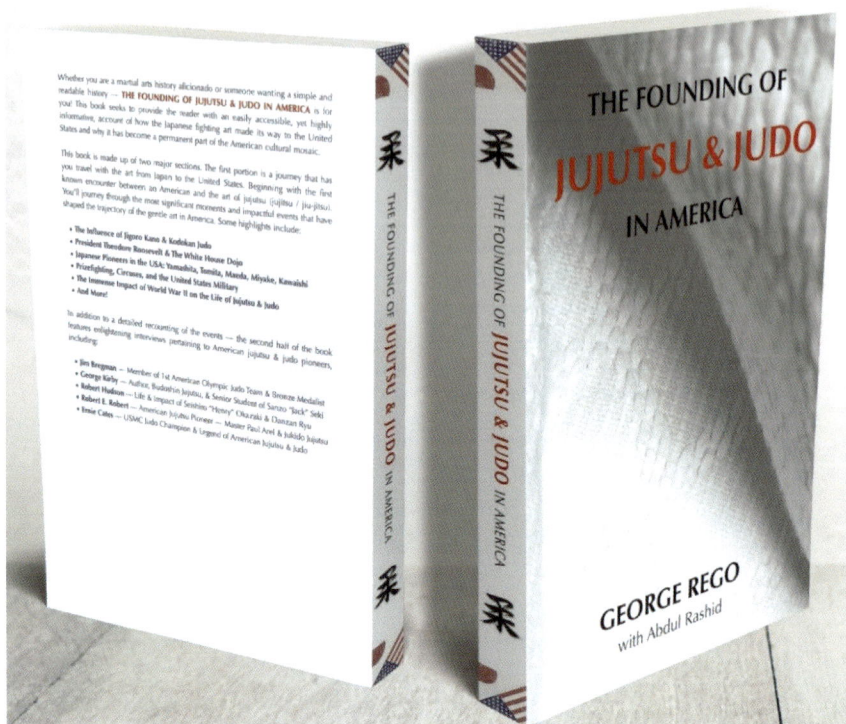

Whether you are a martial arts history aficionado or someone wanting a simple and readable history — THE FOUNDING OF JUJUTSU & JUDO IN AMERICA is for you! This book seeks to provide you an easily accessible, yet highly informative, account of how the Japanese fighting art made its way to the United States and why it has become a permanent part of the American cultural mosaic.

This book is made up of two major sections. The first portion is a journey that has you travel with the art from Japan to the United States. Beginning with the first known encounter between an American and the art of jujutsu (jujitsu / jiu-jitsu).

You'll journey through the most significant moments and impactful events that shaped the trajectory of the art in America. Some highlights include:

- The Influence of Jigoro Kano & Kodokan Judo

- President Theodore Roosevelt & The White House Dojo

- Japanese Pioneers in the USA: Yamashita, Tomita, Maeda, Miyake, Kawaishi

- Prizefighting, Circuses, & the United States Military

- The Impact of World War II & It's Reshaping Jujutsu & Judo

- And more!

In addition to a detailed recounting of the events - the second half of the book features enlightening interviews pertaining to American jujutsu & judo pioneers, including:

- Jim Bregman • Member of 1st American Olympic Judo Team & Bronze Medalist

- George Kirby • Prolific Author, Budoshin Jujutsu, & Senior Student of Sanzo "Jack" Seki

- Robert Hudson • On the Life & Legacy of Seishiro "Henry" Okazaki & Danzan Ryu

- Robert E. Robert • On of His Teacher - American Jujutsu & Karate Pioneer, Master Paul Arel

- Ernie Cates • US Marine Corps Judo Champion & Legend of American Jujutsu & Judo

The founding of Jujutsu, Judo & Aikido in the United Kingdom

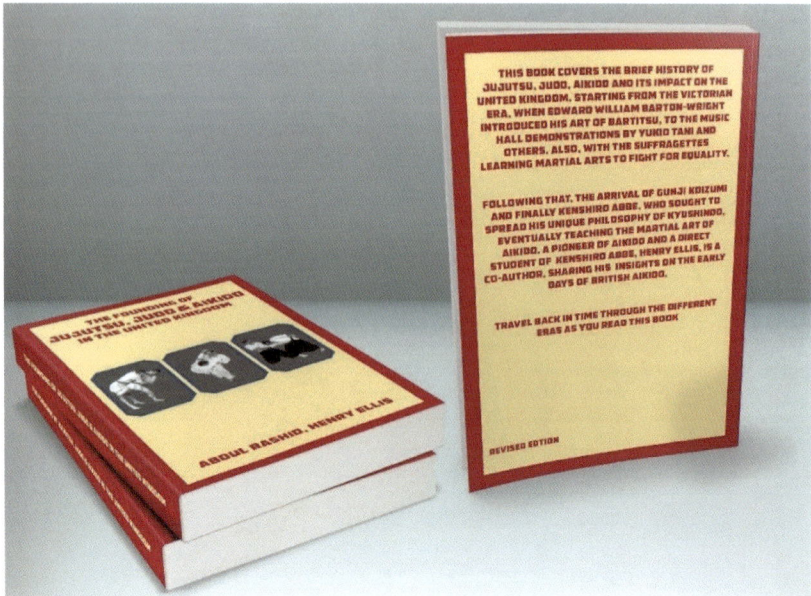

This book covers the brief history of Jujutsu, Judo, Aikido, and its impact on the United Kingdom. Starting from the Victorian era when Edward William Barton-Wright introduced his art of Bartitsu. To the music hall demonstrations by Yukio Tani and others. Also, with the suffragettes learning martial arts to fight for equality. Following that, the arrival of Gunji Koizumi and finally Kenshiro Abbe, who sought to spread his unique philosophy of Kyushindo, eventually teaching the martial art of Aikido. A pioneer of Aikido and a direct student of Kenshiro Abbe, Henry Ellis, is a co-author, sharing his Insights on the early days of British Aikido. Travel back in time through the different eras as you read this book.

British Aikido History

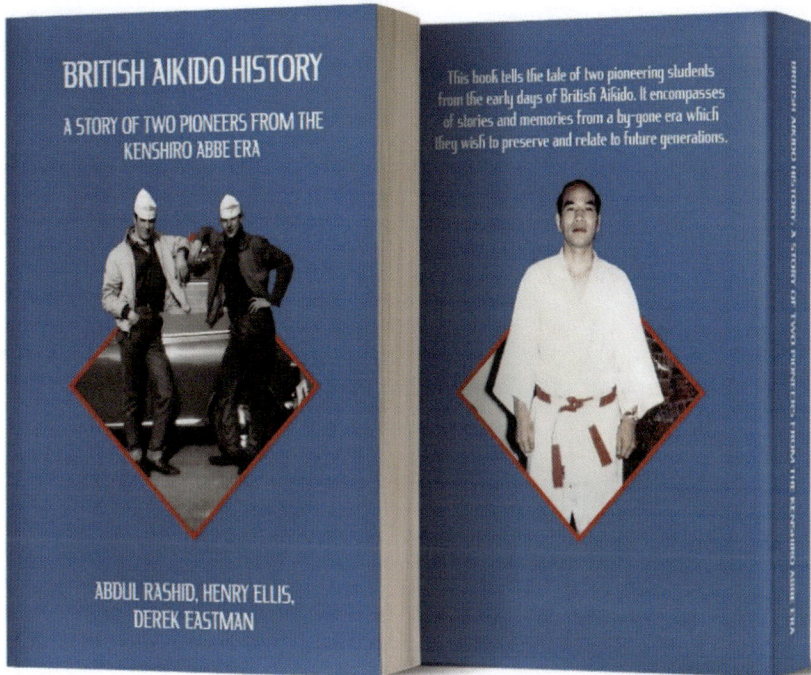

This book tells the tale of two pioneering students from the early days of British Aikido. It encompasses stories and memories from a by-gone era which they wish to preserve and relate to future generations.

Kenshiro Abbe: The Forgotten Budoka

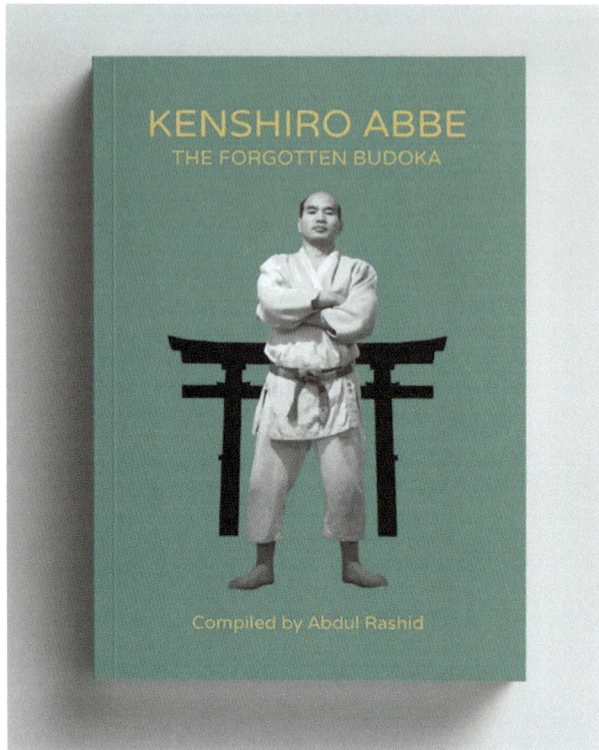

This book uncovers the early life of Kenshiro Abbe, who was known for his proficiency in Judo among other martial arts. He was one of the few that beat the great Masahiko Kimura. This writing delves into his time as a student at the then prestigious Busen college in the early 1930s, progressing as he climbed the ladder competing, rising to fame, becoming an instructor, and joining the Imperial army. Travel back in time as you read the story of a Budoka from a bygone era.

Jim Bregman: An Advocate for American Judo

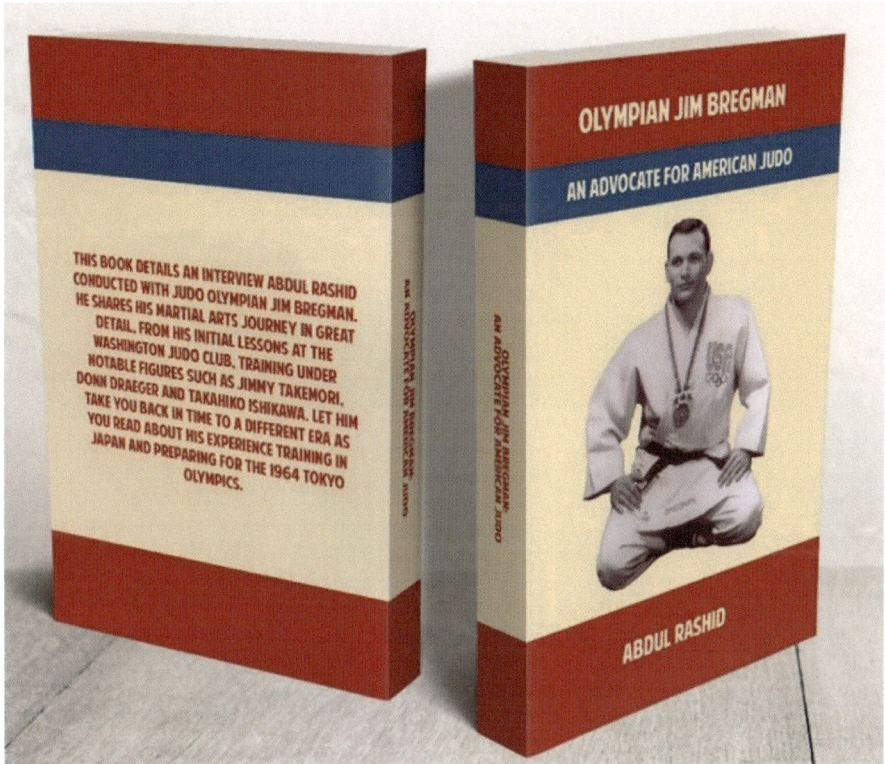

This book details an interview that Abdul Rashid conducted with Judo Olympian Jim Bregman. He shares his martial arts journey in great detail, from his initial lessons at the Washington Judo Club, training under notable figures such as Jimmy Takemori, Donn Draeger and Takahiko Ishikawa. Let him take you back in time to a different era as you read about his experience training in Japan and preparing for the 1964 Tokyo Olympics.

Is Aikido a Martial Art?

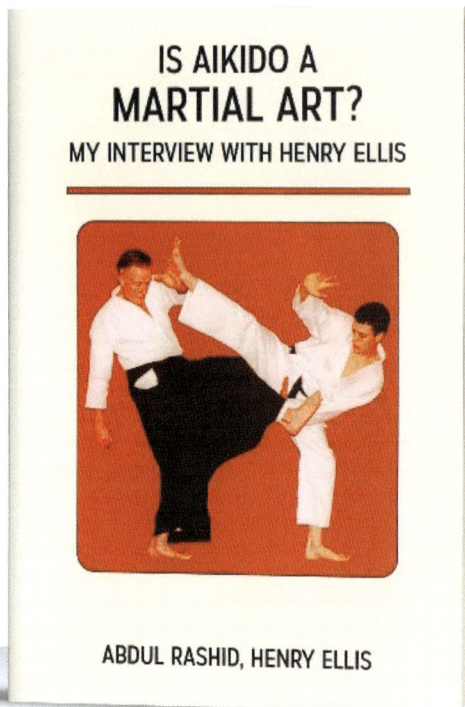

Is Aikido a martial art? This book consists of an interview that I conducted with Henry Ellis, a pioneer of Aikido in the UK since the 1950s. With over 60 years of experience in Aikido, he shares his view on the above topic. Warmups with Karate style kicks and punches, daily runs, full contact training, read about what he went through under the direction of Kenshiro Abbe and Ken Williams at the famous "Hut Dojo". You will have a different perception of Aikido after reading this book.

The British Budo Controversy

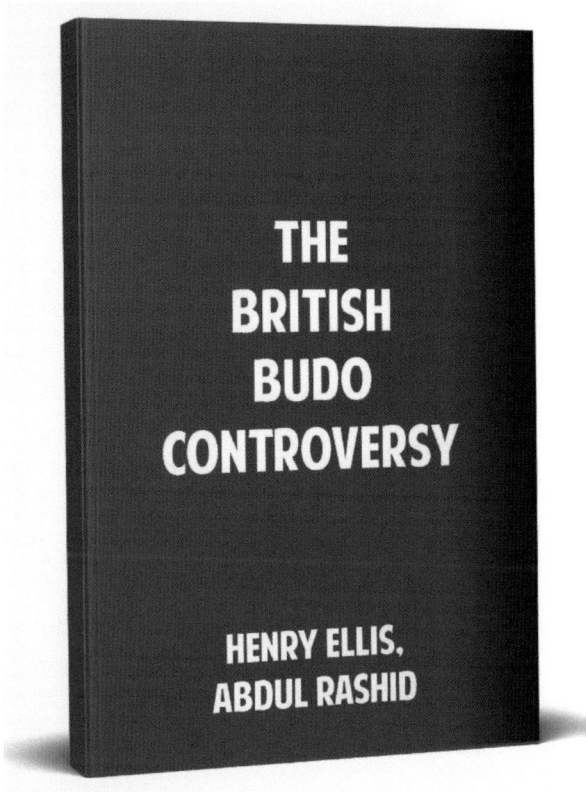

This book delves into the controversy surrounding the history of British Budo. Included in this book are numerous documents and accounts that dispel the myths and claims of the infamous British Aikido Board and Jack Poole.

This page is intentionally left blank.

References/Bibliography

Sources

1) Emil Farkas, 2021, *Bruce Tegner – The Forgotten Pioneer of American Martial Arts*, USAdojo. Available at: https://www.usadojo.com/bruce-tegner-the-forgotten-pioneer-of-american-martial-arts/

2) S Vinaya Kumar, Premkumar Panicker, 2020, *Remembering Bruce Tegnér (1929 – 1985)*, Self Defense Trivandrum. Available at: https://selfdefensetrivandrum.wordpress.com/2020/09/19/remembering-bruce-tegner-1929-1985/

3) Gene Freese, 2017, *Classic Movie Fight Scenes: 75 Years of Bare Knuckle Brawls, 1914-1989*, McFarland. Available at: https://books.google.com/books?id=79g1DwAAQBAJ&dq=june+tegner&source=gbs_navlinks_s

Pictures

All images are copyrighted to their respective owners.

Bruce Tegner dedication photo: *Bruce-Tegner*, 2021, Emil Farkas, USAdojo < https://www.usadojo.com/bruce-tegner-the-forgotten-pioneer-of-american-martial-arts/>

Bruce Tegner signature: *Instant Self-Defence*, n.d, Rodney, eBay <https://www.ebay.com/itm/266182621976?>

Figure 1: *Bruce Tegner young portrait*, 2023, Woolson Holly

Figure 2: *Tegner and father speed ball*, 2023, Woolson Holly

Figure 3: *Tegner and father together*, 2023, Woolson Holly

Figure 4: *Harry Hawelka portrait*, 2023, Woolson Holly

Figure 5: *Marjorie June Tegner portrait*, 2023, Woolson Holly

Figure 6: *June Tegner and Kuwashima*, 2009, Keehan John, John Keehan <http://johnkeehan.blogspot.com/2009/05/timeline-of-martial-arts-in-america.html>

Figure 7: *June Tegner outside Chicago Judo Club*, 2023, Woolson Holly

Figure 8: *June Tegner and members of Chicago Judo Club*, 2023, Woolson Holly

Figure 9: *June portrait*, 2023, Woolson Holly

Figure 10: *Kuwashima portrait*, 2020, Kumar Vinaya, Self Defense Trivandrum <https://selfdefensetrivandrum.wordpress.com/2020/09/19/remembering-bruce-tegner-1929-1985/>

Figure 11: *Tegner Judo Club Chicago*, 1952, Carvalho Danilo, Scribd
<https://www.scribd.com/document/124896941/62127435-Judo-1952#>

Figure 12: *Joe Alai and Jon Tegner*, 1952, Carvalho Danilo, Scribd
<https://www.scribd.com/document/124896941/62127435-Judo-1952#>

Figure 13: *Jon Tegner and John Madrid*, 1952, Carvalho Danilo, Scribd
<https://www.scribd.com/document/124896941/62127435-Judo-1952#>

Figure 14: *Joe Tegner and Edward W. Row*, 1952, Carvalho Danilo, Scribd
<https://www.scribd.com/document/124896941/62127435-Judo-1952#>

Figure 15: *June Tegner Kani Basami*, 1938, Evening Star, Library of Congress
<https://chroniclingamerica.loc.gov/lccn/sn83045462/1938-10-30/ed-1/seq-103/#date1=1777&index=0&rows=20&words=June+Tegner&searchType=basic&sequence=0&state=&date2=1963&proxtext=june+tegner&y=15&x=9&dateFilterType=yearRange&page=1>

Figure 16: *June Tegner ankle lock*, 1938, Evening Star, Library of Congress
<https://chroniclingamerica.loc.gov/lccn/sn83045462/1938-10-30/ed-1/seq-103/#date1=1777&index=0&rows=20&words=June+Tegner&searchType=basic&sequence=0&state=&date2=1963&proxtext=june+tegner&y=15&x=9&dateFilterType=yearRange&page=1>

Figure 17: *The Tegners and Bob Hope*, 2023, Woolson Holly

Figure 18: *Bogart Learns Judo From Woman Expert*, 1949, Toledo union journal, Library of Congress <https://chroniclingamerica.loc.gov/lccn/sn82007637/1949-04-22/ed-1/seq-5/#date1=1777&index=1&rows=20&words=June+Tegner&searchType=basic&sequence=0&state=&date2=1963&proxtext=+june+tegner&y=0&x=0&dateFilterType=yearRange&page=1>

Figure 19: *Top Woman Judo Expert Tosses Hollywood Stars*, 1947, The Wilmington morning star, Library of Congress <https://chroniclingamerica.loc.gov/lccn/sn78002169/1947-01-22/ed-1/seq-6/#date1=1777&index=0&rows=20&words=Judo+June+Tegner&searchType=basic&sequence=0&state=&date2=1963&proxtext=june+tegner+Judo&y=0&x=0&dateFilterType=yearRange&page=1>

Figure 20: *June Tegner and Groucho Marx*, 2023, Woolson Holly

Figure 21: *The Tegners, Bob Hope and Teru Shimada*, 2023, Woolson Holly

Figure 22: JUDO AND JIU-JITSU INSTRUCTIONAL FILM, 1948, Library of Congress, Google Books <https://books.google.com.sg/books?id=yk8hAQAAIAAJ&dq=june+tegner&source=gbs_navlinks_s&redir_esc=y>

Figure 23: *Young Carol Tegner*, 1952, Carvalho Danilo, Scribd <https://www.scribd.com/document/124896941/62127435-Judo-1952#>

Figure 24: *Oops, Mama!*, 1943, The Waterbury Democrat, Library of Congress <https://chroniclingamerica.loc.gov/lccn/sn82014085/1943-02-15/ed-1/seq-1/#date1=1777&index=4&rows=20&words=June+Tegner&searchType=basic&sequence=0&state=&date2=1963&proxtext=+june+tegner&y=0&x=0&dateFilterType=yearRange&page=1>

Figure 25: *Carol and Bruce Tegner*, 2023, Woolson Holly

Figure 26: *Carol Tegner vital points*, 2023, Woolson Holly

Figure 27: *Carol Tegner kuzushi*, 2023, Woolson Holly

Figure 28: *Carol Tegner weapon defense*, 2023, Woolson Holly

Figure 29: *Carol throws Bruce*, 2023, Woolson Holly

Figure 30: *Carol Tegner and James Widenot*, 2016, Adolph Christine, Valley Times <http://www.valleytimes.org/valley-women-carol-tegner-teen-Judo-instructor/>

Figure 31: *Carol Tegner and George Cruse*, 2016, Adolph Christine, Valley Times <http://www.valleytimes.org/valley-women-carol-tegner-teen-Judo-instructor/>

Figure 32: *Carol Tegner throws Allen Smith*, 2016, Adolph Christine, Valley Times <http://www.valleytimes.org/valley-women-carol-tegner-teen-Judo-instructor/>

Figure 33: *Carol Tegner intro on "What's My Line?"*, 2015, What's My Line?, YouTube <https://www.youtube.com/watch?v=--N24ztac70&list=PLqsaqh5sqUxr7GdOOjBQGXR_d7tx0TJ50&index=79>

Figure 34: *Carol Tegner and John Charles Daly*, 2015, What's My Line?, YouTube <https://www.youtube.com/watch?v=--N24ztac70&list=PLqsaqh5sqUxr7GdO0jBQGXR_d7tx0TJ50&index=79>

Figure 35: *Shozo Kuwashima dedication*, 1969, BRUCE TEGNER METHOD OF SELF-DEFENSE, Tegner Bruce

Figure 36: *Bruce Tegner blackbelt certificate*, 2023, Woolson Holly

Figure 37: *Marine Wins Second Judo Expert Award*, 2023, Woolson Holly

Figure 38: *Bruce Tegner at Camp Roberts*, 2023, Woolson Holly

Figure 39: *Bruce Tegner transfer request*, 2023, Woolson Holly

Figure 40: *Bruce Tegner transfer approval*, 2023, Woolson Holly

Figure 41: *Bruce Tegner discharge letter*, 2023, Woolson Holly

Figure 42: *A. B. Lee and Bruce Tegner*, 1952, Carvalho Danilo, Scribd <https://www.scribd.com/document/124896941/62127435-Judo-1952#>

Figure 43: *Bruce Tegner instructing hand-to-hand combat*, 2021, Farkas Emil, USAdojo <https://www.usadojo.com/bruce-tegner-the-forgotten-pioneer-of-american-martial-arts/>

Figure 44: *Bruce Tegner honorary black belt*, 1970, Black Belt Magazine, Google Books <https://books.google.com/books?id=gc4DAAAAMBAJ&dq=bruce+tegner&source=gbs_navlinks_s>

Figure 45: *Chojiro Tani portrait*, 2020, Chojiro Tani Soke. Founder of Shukokai Karate Do. 1920 - 1998, Facebook <https://www.facebook.com/157448704301199/photos/a.1574 53540967382/157453544300715/?type=3>

Figure 46: *Bruce Tegner breaking boards*, 2021, Farkas Emil, USAdojo <https://www.usadojo.com/bruce-tegner-the-forgotten-pioneer-of-american-martial-arts/>

Figure 47: *Tegner in his Hollywood dojo*, 2021, Farkas Emil, USAdojo <https://www.usadojo.com/bruce-tegner-the-forgotten-pioneer-of-american-martial-arts/>

Figure 48: *Tegner Karate class advert*, 2022, Karate Hack, YouTube <https://www.youtube.com/watch?v=wqf17S8C2HE>

Figure 49: *Tegner Yawara advert*, nd, Unclecheesey, eBay, <https://www.ebay.com/itm/325544087396>

Figure 50: *Bruce Tegner advert*, 2023, Woolson Holly

Figure 51: *Bruce Tegner business cards*, 2023, Woolson Holly

Figure 52: BRUCE LEE'S PERSONAL COPY OF THE OPEN HAND AND FOOT FIGHTING, 2012, Julien's Live <https://www.julienslive.com/lot details/index/catalog/79/lot/31345>

Figure 53: *Bruce Lee's Signed Copy*, 2012, Julien's Live <https://www.julienslive.com/lot details/index/catalog/79/lot/31345>

Figure 54: *Judo For Fun: Sports Techniques Made Easy*, n,d, Legitwidgets ,eBay <https://www.ebay.com/itm/285023767943>

Figure 55: *Aikido Self Defense: Holds & Locks for Modern Use*, 2013, Bruce Tegner, Facebook <https://www.facebook.com/139740806183545/photos/a.159 253800898912/159253837565575/?comment_id=224116074937 4863>

Figure 56: *Savate: French Foot Fighting*, 1970, Tegner Bruce, Amazon <https://www.amazon.in/Savate-French-Fighting-Tegner-Bruce/dp/0874070023>

Figure 57: *Libro Completo De karate*, 1990, Tegner Bruce, Archive <https://archive.org/details/librocompletodek0000tegn>

Figure 58: *Bruce Tegner and Alice McGrath*, 2023, Woolson Holly

Figure 59: *Bruce Tegner and Alice McGrath informal shot*, 2023, Woolson Holly

Figure 60: *Alice McGrath and Tegner*, 1969, Self Defense for Girls, YouTube

< https://youtu.be/wpZeBHqirt0?si=Yk2D0EYQc8nB_LxK>

Figure 61: Joan Crawford, Tegner, and Constance Ford, nd, Joan Crawford Best <http://www.joancrawfordbest.com/63caretakers12apr1.htm>

Figure 62: Joan Crawford and Tegner, nd, Joan Crawford Best <http://www.joancrawfordbest.com/63caretakers12apr1.htm>

Figure 63: Gloria Talbott and Tegner, 1959, EMoviePoster <http://auctions.emovieposter.com/Bidding.taf?_function=d etail&Auction_uid1=3045752>

Figure 73: *International Karate Championships 1964 Poster,* 2014, PBA Galleries <https://www.pbagalleries.com/view-auctions/catalog/id/321/lot/98451/Official-Program-featuring-Bruce-Lee-s-Karate-Debut-at-the-International-Karate-Championships-Los-Angles-i-e-Long-Beach-1964-plus-1965-program>

Figure 74: *Bruce Lee one-inch punch,* 2020, Raymond Charles, ScreenRant <https://screenrant.com/bruce-lee-one-inch-punch-explained/>

Figure 75: *Parker and Lee,* 2020, JesúsBajo St, YouTube <https://www.youtube.com/watch?v=Vgo9Ri_yOmg>

Figure 76: *Lee and Coburn,* 2022, Luck Richard, Twitter <https://mobile.twitter.com/RMGLUCK2017/status/1593523534428504065/photo/1>

Figure 77: *Lee and Sharon Tate,* 2019, Loi Lak, JDKLondon <https://www.jkdlondon.com/roman-polanski-thought-bruce-lee-killed-sharon-tate/>

Figure 78: *Bruce Tegner's Complete Book of Judo Paperback Martial Arts Book Vintage 1967,* n.d, pinklucy7494, Ebay <https://www.ebay.com/itm/125404251581>

Figure 79: *Bruce Tegner jump front kick,* 2023, Woolson Holly

Figure 80: *Bruce Tegner jump side kick,* 2023, Woolson Holly

Figure 81: *Bruce Tegner and Anton Geesink,* 2023, Woolson Holly

Figure 82: *Tegner Judo throw,* 2021, Farkas Emil, USAdojo <https://www.usadojo.com/bruce-tegner-the-forgotten-pioneer-of-american-martial-arts/>

Figure 83: *Bruce Tegner jumping knee*, 2023, Woolson Holly

Figure 84: *Bruce Tegner's Complete Book of Jukado Self Defense*, 1970, Tegner Bruce, Amazon <https://www.amazon.ca/Complete-Jukado-Self-defence-Bruce-Tegner/dp/0552084565>

Figure 85: *Bruce Tegner multiple attackers*, 2023, Woolson Holly

Figure 86: *Bob Rosenbaum portrait*, 2020, Kumar Vinaya, Self Defense Trivandrum < https://selfdefensetrivandrum.wordpress.com/2020/09/20/remembering-bruce-tegner-part-2/>

End

Printed in Great Britain
by Amazon

40927001R00087